how2become

A Police Dog Handler
The Insider's Guide

Orders: Please contact How2become Ltd, Suite 2, 50 Churchill Square Business Centre, Kings Hill, Kent ME19 4YU.

You can also order via the e mail address info@how2become. co.uk.

ISBN: 978-1-909229-03-7

First published 2012

Typeset for How2become Ltd by Molly Hill, Canada.

Printed in Great Britain for How2become Ltd by Bell & Bain Ltd, 303 Burnfield Road, Thornliebank, Glasgow G46 7UQ.

CONTENTS

HISTORY OF THE BRITISH POLICE DOG

The strength of the dog has been used to mankind's advantage throughout history. The dog, being naturally stronger than the human being, was often used in some of the earliest battles.

With regards to the police dog, the earliest reports of dogs being used can be traced back to the 15th Century. It is believed that during this time dogs accompanied Parish Constables when they went out to patrol the streets, especially during the evenings. However, it is argued that these dogs were used as pets to provide companionship for the Parish Constables, rather than playing any significant police role in combating crime.

Throughout our history dogs have been used by mankind for a number of reasons, often to perform tasks such as hunting, tracking, guarding, hauling, companionship and communicating. The earliest recorded evidence of this is the Greeks, who used dogs during their battles over 2,500 years ago, and likewise the Romans who used war dogs and these dogs were even given armour.

As for the police dog itself, an early record of what can vaguely be described as a police dog can be traced back to 1859 when police officers in Luton had acquired a bloodhound and used the dog for tracking purposes in their attempt to solve a murder.

As police forces started to develop in the United Kingdom it became common practice for officers to take their own dogs with them on evening patrols, however this was mainly for protection and company. The lack of training given to these dogs meant that their use in reducing and stopping crime was limited. However, the use of dogs in this way was

CHAPTER I
HISTORY OF THE POLICE DOG

As by way of an introduction to your career as a police dog handler this chapter is going to examine the brief history of the police dog within the police service. Each individual police force has its own history describing how the police dog has come to exist in its current role.

It is not possible to cover the history of every police force in this guide and, therefore, this chapter will explore the history of the police dog at a national level. In addition, this chapter will also explore the history of the police dog within the Metropolitan Police Service (MPS). The reason for this is that the MPS are the largest employers of police dog handlers out of all the forces in the United Kingdom.

Before applying for the role of a police dog handler you should research the history of the police dog within your particular force as this will indicate that you have thought carefully about the role you are applying for.

not received well in all forces, and in 1870 the Chief Constable of Northumberland informed his Superintendents to suspend any officer who was found on duty with their dog. This restriction was not lifted until 1910.

Arguably the first use of a dog within the police force can be traced back to the 1880s where a gentleman by the name of Sir Charles Warren used a Blood Hound to try and help solve the Jack the Ripper Murders. However, in this case a rather unfortunate incident occurred in which one of the dogs bit the Commissioner and they both ran off, requiring a police search to find them again. As a result of this, dogs were not given a proper chance to show their abilities at this time.

In the 1890s the Hyde Park police station had a Fox Terrier called Topper who often joined officers on their evening patrols. It has been suggested that the use of the Fox Terrier was probably no more than a publicity stunt for the MPS. Despite his affection from members of the public, Topper was untrained, often ineffective and unpopular with other officers. The development of the police dog within the police force was slow and gradual within the UK Police Force but there was a different story developing on the continent.

THE DEVELOPMENT OF POLICE DOG ABROAD

The story on the police dog in other countries during this time was quite different to that of the UK. One of the first major steps in the development of the police dog on the continent came during the 1890s in Germany where attempts were made to introduce recognised training programmes for the dogs. In 1897, Franz Laufer, a Prussian Police Inspector, had the idea of using dogs to accompany his officers to ward off any attackers. The idea had occurred to him after a number of attacks on Police Officers during their night shift.

At first, his fellow police officers were somewhat sceptical, mainly because Laufer had no previous experience of dogs. Despite this he continued to pursue the idea and in 1900 the Government provided him with a grant to purchase 3 dogs to accompany officers on the patrols. As he was entering new ground there were no guides or books or experts to assist him in this task.

He eventually found a Police Sergeant who had worked with dogs in his previous employment as a gamekeeper. The gamekeeper's name was Sergeant Lange and his initial response was that an Alsatian or German Shepherd Dog would be best suited to the task. Franz, on the other hand, believed that the Great Dane would be more intimidating to the criminals and therefore act as more of a deterrent.

Laufer had a strong belief that the dogs could be used not only for protecting the Police on their patrols, but also for tracking criminals from the scene of a crime. In 1901 his first dog, a Great Dane called Caesar joined the police service. He was kept muzzled and always remained on a lead and others soon followed his recruitment. Local people were dubious, but when one of the dogs tracked a criminal over two miles the dogs and Inspector Laufer got some well-earned publicity.

Further progress was made in 1899 with the formation of the German Shepherd Dog Society, and in 1903 they held police dog trials that demonstrated control, criminal work and various scent exercises. Although the police authorities were impressed with what that had been shown they did not believe that the cost involved in training the dogs justified the results.

Similar developments had also take place in the town of Ghent in Belgium where the Police Chief, Mr Van-Wesemael, was leading the way in the employment of police dogs as

early as 1859. This forward thinking Police Chief was also using dogs to accompany his officers on patrol at night. He used Belgium Sheepdogs which could be well trained and were found to be highly effective.

He believed that the police dog possessed a number of qualities that made them effective in combating crime. Firstly, he believed they would be more cost effective than increasing the number of police officers on patrol. Secondly, he believed that the police dogs could follow a suspect more quickly than a police officer. Dogs are also equipped with a greater sense of hearing and scent which means they can search a place without being noticed. The final reason was the agility of the police dog would enable them to chase criminals fleeing a crime scene over various obstacles that may have previously hindered the traditional police officer. Within a short space of time the number of police dogs in Ghent quickly grew to 69.

Other countries such as France, Austria and Hungary soon followed suit with dogs becoming a part of their police services. The dogs were employed at this time to create fear, to act as deterrent and to protect their handler from any potential attack. The breeds most commonly used in Germany and Belgium during this time were Shepherds, Boxers, Dobermans and Airedales.

FURTHER DEVELOPMENTS WITHIN THE UK

In the UK however there was little interest in the use of dogs within the police service until a dog trainer by the name of Colonel Richardson tried to persuade the Police of the benefits of using police dogs. He drew attention to the work, the role and the use of police dogs in countries such as Germany, France and Belgium and suggested

that the Metropolitan Police start its own Dog Section. In 1906 a representative from the force visited France to see how the dogs were being used abroad, but they returned unimpressed.

The same year Mr Geddes, the Chief Goods Manager for Hull Docks in Yorkshire, visited Ghent and happened to see the work of the police dogs. He was very impressed with what he saw and on his return to work arranged a meeting with Superintendent J Dobie of the North Eastern Railway Police who was responsible for policing the docks at Hull. Mr Geedes was able to convince the Police Superintendent that dogs may assist his officers in the security at the docks. On 26th November 1907, the two men and some other officers attended Ghent where they visited the Ghent Police Dog Section. At this time the Police Dog Section had 40 officers and dogs.

Superintendent Dobie was significantly impressed and was determined to set up a similar scheme when he returned to the docks at Hull. As a result of this visit the first Police dogs went on patrol at the Hull docks in 1908. Initially there were just four dogs but on 26th November 1908 the scheme extended to Hartlepool Docks and shortly afterwards to the Tyne Docks and Middlesbrough Docks.

These dogs were only used at night and were probably not specific to an individual handler. They were trained to protect the police uniform and to attack anyone who was not wearing a uniform. Anyone who was not in uniform in the docks at night was considered to be a suspect by the dogs. This even included the dog handlers who were not in their uniform.

In 1910 Major Richardson wrote to every Chief Constable in the country informing them of the success that police

dogs were having abroad and suggested the introduction of police dogs to assist police officers on patrol. He particularly highlighted the ability of the dogs to act as a deterrent to burglars and to capture those trying to escape. Major Richardson was a respected dog trainer from the military and as a result of his advice some Chief Constables took positive steps to implement police dogs.

In 1913 Major Llewellyn Atcherely, the Chief Constable of the West Riding of Yorkshire, expressed his support for any officers wishing to train dogs to assist them as the role of the police dog began to develop. A year later, Major Richardson addressed the members of Chief Constable Association during which he highlighted the benefits of using police dogs and also classified the police dog into two types, the night patrol dog and the criminal tracking dog (which had the sole purpose of tracking down criminals).

The achievements of trained police dogs in Ghent, Belgium quickly spread to several other countries, and by World War I, dogs were being trained to perform specific military duties, as messengers, guards and sentries. The German shepherd was used extensively by the Germans on the Western Front and attracted attention both in England and the United States. The good work of these police dogs became known to the military and during the early months of the World War ten police dogs from Hull Docks were conscripted into the army.

Following the success of the police dogs at Hull Docks, they were sent to other railway company police forces around the country. One of the first dogs was called "Charlie" who was on patrol with his handler PC Easton when they came across a man armed with a knife. The officer attempted to arrest the man but was stabbed in the chest and his police dog then

leapt on the man to defend his trainer and held him down until he was arrested.

During the War the work of the Police Dog Section at Hull continued to develop back home under the direction of Inspector Dobson. By the end of the War no less than 185 suspects had been arrested at the docks, many with the assistance of the police dogs. Yet despite this, many police forces still showed little interest in the use dogs within the force following the end of the War in 1918.

For a dog to obtain the title of "Police Dog" they had to be trained to complete a total of 83 exercises to a high standard. In the early 1920s a number dog breeds were tried and tested including the Great Dane, the Bull Mastiff, the Retriever, the Doberman and the Mastiff. After the First World War the Dog Section at Hull came under review in 1923 and the dog trainers decided to use Alsatians as police dogs.

The dog had originally been used by the German Army during the war and although the Alsatian became a popular breed by the mid 1920s it was still new to Britain and was often treated with suspicion. The Bull Mastiff was also a popular breed of dog with a good tracking nose and in 1925 the National Bull Mastiff Police Dog Club was created.

However, it took until the late 1920s for other "non-railway" Police Forces to become interested in the use of police dogs and it wasn't until 1934 that the Home Office set up a committee to evaluate their use and their training facilities. It was initially felt that dogs on the streets would harm police/public relations but after considering a report on the use of police dogs on the continent the decision was made to carry out experiments in the breeding and training of police dogs.

The following year the Inspector of Constabulary agreed

that the MPS could have two Labradors which commenced patrol in 1938 on the streets of Brixton and Southwark. The initial experiments came to an end with the outbreak of the Second World War and the two Labradors introduced into the MPS were handed over to the Cheshire Constabulary.

During the Second World War the number of dogs being used within the police force reduced significantly. One of the main reasons for this was that in 1940 all dogs in the United Kingdom were invited to register for national service. Following their involvement in the First World War only certain breeds were recruited, but the duties ranged from mine detection to guarding buildings. For a dog to be enlisted with the army they had to pass an intensive training course with those successful dogs being shipped out to serve in the army and the unsuccessful ones returned to their homes.

Following the end of Second World War the interest in use of dogs within the police force was renewed due to the rising crime rates in London and in 1946 the MPS acquired four Labrador puppies for training. It was decided at this point that for the training to be successful each dog would be appointed one police handler and that the dog would live with that person.

In 1947 the Chief Constable of Surrey, Joseph Simpson, had become interested in the training and development of dogs for police work. Mr Simpson enlisted the help of PC Darbyshire, who was working for Scotland Yard at the time and had previously shown little interest in the Metropolitan Police Dog Section as they were using Labradors. PC Darbyshire, who favoured the use of the Alsatian as a police dog, was instructed to develop a police dog section for Surrey Police based on the Continental approach to dog training and breeding.

On the 27th September 1950 Surrey opened its own Police Dog training school at Mount-Browne, Guildford. Within the space of four years the majority of the large police forces in the UK had established dog sections and the number of police dogs being used grew at a rapid rate. In 1955 it was agreed between the dog schools that a training programme was required to fully develop the dog and to make the best use of their qualities for police work. The training programme was to pay particular attention to the searching, tracking and control of the dog.

In 1958 this was taken up by the Home Office Committee on Police Dogs whose purpose was to guide and provide advice on a national level. During the 1960s there were a number of significant developments that pushed forward the role of the dog within the police force. In 1963 a training manual was produced entitled "Police dogs – Training and Care" and in 1964 a National Course for instructors was created.

THE DEVELOPMENT OF SPECIALIST POLICE DOGS

As the role of the police began to grow within the police force so did the demand for specialist dogs. The role of the police had evolved from its original position of simply accompanying officers on night patrols to playing an active role in capturing criminals and acting as a deterrent. These were often referred to, and are still referred to, as general purpose police dogs. However, as society changed so did the types of crimes that were committed, and as the type of police work changed so did the demand for specialist police dogs.

Originally specialist police dogs were selected from the ranks of general police dogs on a performance basis. The problem was that these police dogs were performing two roles, and the two roles often conflicted and contrasted with

each other. They were not only required to carry out their normal duties in searching for criminals, but then to switch to a specific scent such as that of a particular substance. The decision was then made to introduce and train police dogs for one specific role and deploy them as and when they were required.

DRUG DETECTION DOG

The first type of specialised dog is the drug detection dog and these are specifically trained to search a place, building or individual for the scent of particular drugs. By focusing on one particular scent it enables the police dog to be more effectively trained and therefore perform to a higher standard when on duty. In many countries, these types of dogs are used in airports to sniff the baggage/people passing through the airport for illegal substances and they are often trained to follow a simple command such as sitting down if they do detect any substances. The first drug detection dog in the UK was a Metropolitan Police Dog called Rex in 1953 who was trained by his handler PC Arthur Holman. In the beginning the drug detection dog was simply trained to detect the drug cannabis, but today these dogs are trained to detect all the common types of drugs.

EXPLOSIVE DETECTION DOG

The second type of specialist dog is the explosive detection dog which is trained to detect the scent of explosives. Today these dogs work very closely with the bomb disposal team and form an essential part of the police force. The position of this type of dog within the police developed out of a fear of political extremists in 1968 and the safety of Prince Charles. At this time the Chief Constable of South Wales,

Melbourne Thomas believed that if police dogs could be trained to detect the scent of drugs then surely the same principle could be applied to the scent of explosives. A training programme was soon introduced to try and train a dog for this specific purpose. PC Sydenham and his Labrador worked closely with the Chester bomb disposal and after an intensive training regime the Labrador was brought into active service.

BURIED BODY DETECTION DOG

The late 1970s saw the introduction of another specialised police dog, one capable of detecting buried bodies. The first buried body detection dogs were a Border Collie called Tess and an Alsatian called Carl. They both underwent an 18 month training programme at the Lancashire Dog Training school in 1969. The primary use of these dogs is for the detection of human remains and they now play a vital role in helping the police solve murder cases. During their training these dogs are taught to detect the remains of pigs as opposed to real human remains as it is believed the scent of pig remains closely resembles that of human remains.

THE DEVELOPMENT WITHIN THE METROPOLITAN POLICE FORCE

The MPS introduced 172 dogs of different breeds to accompany officers on patrol in 1914, but it was not until 1938 that two Labradors, who were patrolling in Peckham at the time, could be described as the first "real" police dogs within the MPS. However, it wasn't until after the Second World War that role of the police dog within the MPS began to gain momentum.

Shortly after the Second World War had finished six

Labradors were introduced as a way of combating crime and two years later, in 1948, the first German Shepherd dog was used. The German Shepherd is now the most recognised police dog and its date of introduction is a key point to remember.

Over the next couple of years the number of police dogs within the MPS grew as their use and success in combating crime also grew. By 1950 the number had grown to 90 dogs with the Dog section being based at Imber Court. With the growing recognition of the police dog and its role, the number of police dogs being trained at Imber Court rapidly increased, as did the growing number of complaints from local residents concerning the noise levels.

The problem with the training school at Imber Court was that it was also a sports ground used by the Police Athletic Association and the limited space allocated to the dog section meant that there was no specific place allocated for dog training. In addition to this, the kennels were poorly constructed and the only breed of dog being allowed was the Labrador. At this time the Alsatian was still considered as dangerous and unpredictable by the public and many officers.

By 1952 Imber Court had changed its policy and the training school was opened up to other breeds of dog including the Alsatian. As a result of this, Sir Peter Mathews, the then Chief Instructor of dog training for the MPS left Imber Court and headed for Ketson, where all dog training courses still take place today.

The Dog Training Establishment was established in 1954 at Keston surrounded by farmland and miles away from any local residents and comprised of 6 kennels and a wooden shed. It was officially opened in June 1954 by the then

Commissioner, Sir John Nott-Bower. However, after only a week of being opened disaster struck and the training centre had to be closed after an outbreak of Hardpad which killed 19 dogs. It was believed that the disease was brought from Imber Court. The poor design of the kennels and the fact that here was no inoculation program meant that the disease spread with entire litters dying. Today, the site includes 15 acres and over 100 purpose-built hygienic units.

At this time the Dog Training Establishment did not employ kennel staff and as a result of this the responsibility of training the 162 dogs was undertaken by three officers: Station Sgt Mathews, Sgt Boath and Sgt Morphy (who later became the Chief Superintendent in charge of the Metropolitan Police Dog section).

The 1960s led to another turning point in the history of the police dog with the first two police dogs being trained to detect drugs, in this case cannabis. This change arose after Detective Inspector Cooke heard how dogs were being used in South America to search marine vessels for coffee. After he was transferred to the drug squad he asked if two dogs could be trained in a similar way.

Following the initial success in training the police dog to search for cannabis a number of other drugs soon followed. Today certain police dogs are being trained to locate Bank notes. The role of the police dog evolved again during the 1980s and police dogs were now being trained to work with CO19 Firearms and locate human remains.

In December 1989 a terrorist bomb exploded on a 747 which crashed in and around the Scottish town of Lockerbie. Two dog handlers from Scotland arrived on the scene, Davy Connell and Alistair Campbell. The police

dogs played a significant role in aiding the officers to locate a total of 23 bodies.

More recently in 1994, firearm recovery police dogs were introduced into the MPS and today, the MPS has around 250 dog teams across London performing a variety of roles and tasks to help tackle and prevent crime. The value of the modern day police dog has been recognised to such an extent that there are now over 2,500 police dogs amongst the various police forces in the UK, with the Alsatian standing out as the most popular breed for general purpose police dogs.

The MPS also has the largest police dog breeding program in the UK and not only supplies London with police dogs but also provides many other forces with police dogs, especially those that do not have the capabilities or training facilities.

The aim of this chapter was to provide an overview of the history of the police dog with a particular focus on the MPS. The key point to remember from this chapter is that when applying for the role of a police dog handler you will need to have an understanding of history of the police dog on a local level as well as a national level. Therefore it is essential that you research the history of the police dog handler for the force you are applying to. This will demonstrate that you have taken time to research the role you are applying for and will help you stand out from other candidates.

CHAPTER 2
POLICE DOG HANDLER FAQS

What is the standard pay for a police dog handler?

The current rates of pay for police officers can be found here:

http://www.policeservice.co.uk

How soon after joining can I apply to be a dog handler?

After two years later on patrol as a police constable you can apply to train to be a dog handler. You will need to obtain your sergeant's recommendation.

How can I improve my changes of selection?

The competition is tough, as there are only a few dog handlers in each police force. Previous experience working with dogs will help – even time spent in a voluntary capacity could put you above another candidate.

Do you have to be a UK citizen to join the police?

You must be a British citizen, an EC/EEA national or a

Commonwealth citizen or foreign national with no restrictions on your stay in the United Kingdom. Foreign nationals and UK citizens who have lived abroad may have to wait some time for security and vetting clearance. All applicants have to be vetted to the same standard before appointment. (Source: www.policeservice.co.uk)

Can I join the police if I have a criminal record?

The important thing to do is be completely honest during your application. As part of the vetting process the police will carry out extensive checks into your background and financial circumstances to determine whether you have ever been convicted of an offence or been involved in activities that could compromise your integrity.

You may still be eligible to join the police service if you have minor convictions or cautions but there are certain offences and conditions that will make you ineligible including committing a violent crime or a public order offence. Contact your chosen police force for more information.

Can I apply if I have a tattoo?

Current guidelines are that you should not have tattoos which could cause offence to others. Tattoos are also deemed unacceptable *"if they are particularly prominent, garish, offensive or undermine the dignity and authority of your role."*

If you have tattoos on your face, neck, forearms or hands you need to declare it on your application form and describe their exact nature.

Can I apply to become a police officer without a driving licence?

Yes, but you will need to learn to drive and pass your test in

your own time and at your own expense within the first year of being appointed.

What Are The Eyesight Requirements?

The eyesight standards for new Police Officer recruits are:

* Unaided vision (without spectacles or lenses) - 6/36 or better in either eye is required.

* Binocular vision (vision with both eyes) worse than 6/6 requires correction.

* Aided vision (wearing lenses or spectacles) - 6/12 or better in either eye and 6/6 or better using both eyes (binocular vision) is required.

* Near vision - N6 at 40 cm with both eyes together (aided).

Can I Apply If I Have Had Laser Eye Surgery?

If you have undergone Radial Keratotomy, Arcuate Keratotomy or corneal grafts you can't apply. If you have undergone other forms of refractive surgery such as LASIK, LASEK and PRK providing 6 weeks have passed since the surgery, you can.

CHAPTER 3
TYPES OF POLICE DOGS

The police forces use a number of breeds of dogs for a variety of duties. The type of dog sometimes depends on the job to be done, but the following breeds are the ones usually used in Britain:

- German Shepherd
- Rottweiler
- Giant Schnauzer
- Doberman
- Labrador

- Belgian Shepherd
- Springer Spaniels
- Weimaraners
- German Short-Haired Pointers

Searching and tracking are the main tasks of police dogs. A single police officer is no match for a police dog as they are able to search more quickly and in very constricted places.

A dog's nose is one of the best bits of equipment available to the police. A trained sniffer dog's nose can detect

10-year-old smells and is around 2,000 times better than a human's nose. The dog is able to follow a human scent so well that anyone who may be lost or hiding can very quickly be found. Large crowds, especially those who may exhibit bad behaviour, are a good place for dogs to be visible, if only to deter possible incident.

Some dogs are trained specially to search for drugs, explosives and guns. Springer Spaniels and Labradors are often used because they are such excellent trackers. Due to the fact that terrorism has become a very real threat in the present time, these specialist dogs are well used by the police in any area which may be a possible target for terrorists.

Police dogs usually come from two sources. A dog may be given to the police by someone, either as a gift, or because they became too much for the owner to handle. They can be anywhere from 1 to 3 years old. Dogs are also bought from specialist breeders, who raise the special types of dogs used by the police force.

The new dogs must be carefully assessed and must carry out a series of specially designed tests to see if they possess the temperament and skills needed to work with the police. Those that pass the tests will be paired with a handler and they will both go through the beginning course.

Some puppies will be placed with experienced handlers and go through a process to ensure they are raised in a family environment to develop naturally.

If the puppy then continues on the training programme, between 1 and 1.5 years it will begin the general course. The handler chooses the name of the dog, which is often a short name, easily called and understood by the dog.

The dog is trained, whether as an adult or a puppy, to

complete all tasks needed to become a police dog. The handlers kennel the dogs at their own homes to ensure they remain bonded. They even go on holiday together.

Most general police dogs are retired at 7 or 8 years old. Specialist dogs have a longer working life of around 10 years. The handler may choose to keep their dog, but if this is not possible for any reason, the dog is given to a compatible owner for the rest of its life.

GERMAN SHEPHERD

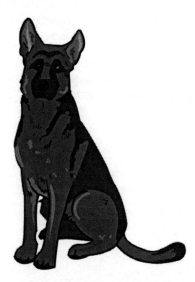

Perhaps the most recognised of these dogs seen working with the police is the German Shepherd. Their dark tan/brown and black colouring and alert pointed ears give a wolf-like appearance, which belies their loyalty and obedience. German Shepherds have been used as working dogs throughout their history because they are so intelligent, agile and strong.

They are beautiful, graceful and fast, willing to guard, protect and please their masters. During World War II German Shepherds were invaluable and used as message dogs and search dogs. They were the first to work for the police as general purpose dogs because of their bravery, intelligence and stamina.

The German Shepherd is eager to learn and responds quickly to training. They excel at tracking, as well as their more recognised talent of chasing and cornering suspects. This dog responds very well to its trainer in a close-bonded relationship. They are self-confident animals, and they respond well to rewards during training that also build on their confidence.

German Shepherds are particularly skilled at the following tasks:

- Searching for missing people or suspects of a crime

- Finding things that may have been hidden or dumped as a suspect has left a crime scene

- Tracking a scent on the ground left by a person

- Chasing and holding a suspect who is running away

- Disarming a suspect who is clearly armed and dangerous

- Controlling crowds that may be hostile

ROTTWEILER

The Rottweiler has perhaps been branded with a bad reputation, due not to their nature, but as a result of some owners' treatment of their dogs. Because they are such large dogs, if they are not trained well and handled properly, they can become very powerful and aggressive. With their short black hair, brown markings, broad head with forward carried ears and a docked tail, they are easily recognisable and sometimes feared.

However, the Rottweiler is a devoted dog with a reliable temperament. They will defend and protect their owners, rewarding their care and training with companionship and loyalty. The dog must be trained when young, as they are such big and powerful animals. The trainer needs to be the pack leader, so that the Rottweiler knows the leader and can obey. The relationship will then be a success and the dog will be content and reliable. When proper training is completed,

the Rottweiler will be good with children, other pets and all humans in their household.

The police use Rottweilers, much as German Shepherds, for general purpose work, which includes search and rescue, chase and apprehend, crowd control, tracking people and finding objects. They are very intelligent animals and are trained to a high calibre of work with the police. Their courage and strength keep them going against all obstacles, yet their loyalty and loving nature makes them worth their weight in gold.

GIANT SCHNAUZER

The Giant Schnauzer is probably not as familiarly known as a police dog. It stands with a square stature, being usually as high as it is long, and with a large head and straight flat head and muzzle. Its coat is wiry and can be black or salt and pepper. The dog has bushy eyebrows, whiskers and a beard, with a large black nose. Usually its tail is docked and the ears can be cropped.

Giant Schnauzers are so loyal and loving that they rarely leave their owner's side. Properly trained, this breed makes a good pet. As with the Rottweiler, the Giant Schnauzer needs to know that its owner is the leader of the pack. Training must be consistent and firm, giving positive feedback and rewards. The Giant Schnauzer is spirited and bold and very

intelligent. They must learn to recognise a variety of people in order to be sociable rather than suspicious. As with most dogs, consistent training is essential in order to have the Giant Schnauzer respond to the trainer as the alpha in the pack. They need very early training and consistent leadership so they can become versatile in all their spheres of work.

Because the Giant Schnauzer is so large, their size may often deter criminals when they are being chased. They have a very large bark as well and can therefore act as excellent guard dogs. Giant Schnauzers were used during the world wars, which was nearly the end of the breed. Their popularity is not great, but they have qualities that make them lovable as well as being very hardworking dogs for the police. Their stubbornness also makes them tenacious and loyal.

DOBERMAN

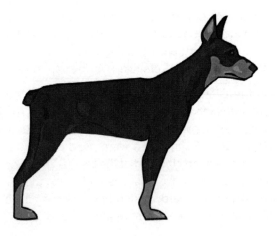

The full name of the Doberman is Doberman Pinscher, and it's very presence is elegant and powerful. It is a muscular dog with short hair, coloured black, black and tan, bluish-grey, red or tan and white. Most people associate Dobermans with being the black strong dogs that appear with the bad guys in films, barking and warning off the good guys. Although tails are usually docked and ears cropped, this practice may now be illegal. The ears are cropped to make them stand up, rather than falling forwards. Without cropped ears and docked tail, the Doberman's ears and tail are similar to a hound's.

Although they have been bred to be guard dogs of a high calibre, Dobermans are very versatile. They are devoted and watchful, and will take excellent care of their owners. They may strike fear in hearts with their watchdog capabilities,

but they are not vicious animals. They are highly intelligent and easy to train, with great energy, stamina and strength. A Doberman loves to be near humans and is very devoted and loyal. Trainers need to be firm, as a Doberman can be pushy if the trainer lets it have its own way.

Consistency and confidence, along with positive reinforcement in training will make the Doberman feel secure. They are known to be very good with children and the elderly, as long as their trainers have taken the alpha position and as long as the dog has sufficient exercise and mental stimulation. The Doberman needs human contact and doesn't like to be left alone.

The Doberman's skills include guarding, tracking, and search and rescue. They are devoted and will defend their owners fearlessly. They can become a one-person dog, but can be trained to include a whole family.

LABRADOR

The English Labrador is a heavy dog, larger than its taller, leaner American cousin. A slightly longer, more muscular dog, the Labrador Retriever is coloured black, yellow or chocolate. Its broad head sits on a powerful neck, with a thick nose and wide muzzle. The Labrador has soft, intelligent eyes and pendant ears and a strong, thick otter-like tail. It also has webbed feet for strong swimming.

This is a dog that is very affectionate and patient, always loyal and willing to please. Its loving nature means it is a dog that likes to play and swim, and that enjoys children and other dogs and animals. A Labrador will bark at new people, but will then welcome them, so they do not make good guard dogs, although they are very watchful. They are easy to train and their patience is a bonus to the trainer's efforts. The Labrador enjoys being led by its trainer, so benefits

most from a trainer who lets the dog know he is the leader of the pack. A dog left without strong leadership or physical and mental exercise may become destructive. Because their necks are so strong, they must be taught not to pull on the lead. The Labrador also needs to be socialised as a puppy in order to be more amenable to strangers.

Labradors are more usually seen as guide dogs for the blind or service dogs for disabled people. Because the Labrador is very good at hunting, tracking, retrieving, narcotics detection and search and rescue, it is an essential worker for the police. Their keen sight and sense of smell makes them excellent 'finders'. Labradors are also used to sniff for drugs in public places and are seldom noticed because they can carry out this task without touching anyone. Because they are friendly dogs, no one suspects that they are being used to sniff for illegal substances.

BELGIAN SHEPHERD DOG

This is a dog which we don't readily associate with police work, but which is regularly used by the police. Also known as the Groenendael, the Belgian Shepherd is black and muscular, agile and proportioned so as to appear very proud. Its ears are erect and triangular and it has a long, tapering muzzle. The Belgian Shepherd has a mid-length coat with a neck ruff and feathering on its belly, legs and tail. It may have a little white on its chest, chin or toes. The feathered tail is long, balancing out the tapered muzzle and deep chest.

There are four Belgian Sheepdogs, and the Groenendael is the most popular. It's a very territorial dog, serious and protective, but also very obedient and intelligent. The Belgian Shepherd may become over-sensitive or shy if not socialised from a puppy. Training must be consistent, firm but not harsh, as this would make the dog uncooperative. Gentle training works best, and the dog learns quickly.

Because they enjoy working and competing, the Belgian Shepherds are excellent police dogs. They have a lot of energy, so need to have work to carry out. The dog bonds well with only one or two people and tend to be overbearing towards other smaller dogs or pets. As their working history is as herders, they can have the habit of circling and nipping at heels. This behaviour needs to be overcome by the trainer. The dog needs to be close to humans, however, and not left to its own devices. It is a good swimmer and has an all-round talent for most types of police work. The Belgian Shepherd has strength of body and character that will defend its owner and seek to please in every way.

SPRINGER SPANIEL

Springer Spaniels are employed by the police in sniffing out explosives, drugs or illegal substances. They are trained to detect these items and will search anywhere and everywhere in order to find them. They can even sniff out drugs on people as they are walking past. As they are small dogs, they can easily fit into tight spaces where other dogs are unable to go. Spaniels are also trained to recover weapons, whether hidden or not. They also specialise in searching for explosives, so can be seen at major VIP functions, especially before the VIPs arrive, in order to ensure that the area is safe.

Smaller than other dog breeds used in policing, the Springer Spaniel is compact and has long ears. Its coat can be liver and white or black and white, often with tan markings. The dog has an expression that seems to melt its owner's heart, with dark eyes and a trusting eagerness that is always alert

and intelligent. The Spaniel can move quickly over rough ground as it works in its searching and recovering process.

The Springer Spaniel is a very active and strong-willed dog. Owners must be prepared to ensure they are given plenty of exercise. The Springer is an affectionate and loving family dog, but if they become bored, problems can arise. They never seem to get tired. The Springer Spaniel's temperament is usually steady and calm, and they are sociable dogs. Because they are such quick and energetic learners, they are bright, skilful and eager to be obedient. It would be hard to find a dog that is more joyful than a Springer, and their bravery is equalled by their loving nature. Springer Spaniels love everyone they meet.

The Springer Spaniel needs early socialisation and training in obedience. Training must be equal parts of determination, justice, consistency and praise. The trainer's careful training will bring the result of a joyful and hardworking companion.

WEIMARANER

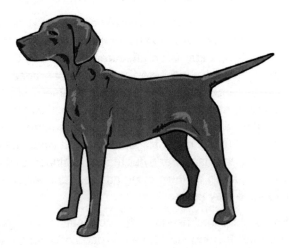

The Weimaraner originates from Germany and it is often named the 'Silver Ghost'. This comes from their grey colouring, anywhere from mousey grey to silver and silvery blue, sometimes with a white-marked chest. They usually have golden eyes, but sometimes they are blue. Their original use is as pointers and retrievers, so they are hardworking dogs that are excellent at hunting, tracking and search and rescue. Weimaraners are agile and possess a wonderful coordination and endurance. They can work for a long time and can track scents from very long distances. They are also excellent guard dogs.

Weimaraners are friendly dogs, very loving and alert. However, it is a large and muscular dog, so although it can work well in a family situation, care must be taken around young children and the elderly. They love being part of a family

and make good companion pets. Their elegance and grace make the Weimaraner a beautiful dog.

Training needs to be firm and will take time and dedication. Weimaraners have a lot of energy, which will make a well-trained dog confident and bold. They must be socialised at an early age in order to not only familiarise them with people and other pets, but to give them the attention they crave. If the Weimaraner is not trained well then they can be a very disruptive influence in a home situation as they are so large and strong. As a result they can be difficult to manage. Weimaraners are very intelligent and eager to please; their quick wit gives them the ability to understand what their trainer asks them to do. The Weimaraner is a dominant breed, and trainers must be confident to overcome their dominance. Well trained, the Weimaraner will be a very useful member of any police team.

GERMAN SHORT-HAIRED POINTER

The German Short-Haired Pointer is also sometimes called the Wire-Haired Pointer. It is an elegant and well-balanced hunting dog, very dignified in its carriage. Its ears are broad and high, lying close to the head. The dog is very muscular and strong, with short hair coloured liver or liver with white spots, black or black and white. Their intelligence is evident in their eyes and in their energetic working at hunting, pointing and retrieving. The Pointer never gets tired and they have no fear of any obstacle they may meet in their work.

The Short-Haired Pointer needs almost constant exercise in order to make it a happy dog. They are never happier than when they are working hard. As they are sturdy and energetic, they are also alert and eager to please their owner. The Pointer is intelligent and affectionate, but does not like being left to its own devices. It needs to know what its job is and exactly how the trainer wants it to carry the job out.

The trainer needs to understand what the Pointer requires in regard to training, so that the dog can be its very best. Early socialisation with other animals and people is needed in order to make the Pointer used to working with them. They love people and are very affectionate, loyal and trustworthy dogs. Owners will find that they take a lot of time to care for properly.

The Pointer can be a very independent and stubborn dog, so training must be firm, consistent and rewards based. They are resourceful workers and will reward their owners and trainers with hard work and results. The police work they undertake is mainly in tracking, search and rescue and retrieving.

In summary, the types of police dogs are varied, but all have in common the following qualities:

- Loyalty to their owners/ trainers
- Endurance
- Strength
- Agility
- Eagerness to please
- Hard working
- Result oriented
- Tireless
- Intelligence
- Energetic
- Affectionate
- Courage.

The police force would be a much less effective organisation without the aid and assistance of its canine colleagues. As the current television programme about police dogs say, "Bring In the Dogs!"

Police dogs have different jobs, according to the breed of dog and each breed's specific skills. Each Police Force uses a variety of types of dogs in order to help them in their work every day.

The main breed is the most recognisable as a police dog, perhaps, and is usually a German Shepherd or Belgian Shepherd dog, used as a General Purpose Dog. This dog is large, has great stamina, works hard, is willing to train and can be taught to control their aggression. Other breeds also used as General Purpose Dogs are the Rottweiler, Doberman and Giant Schnauzer.

The General Purpose Dogs' particular skills include searching for suspects and missing people, locating objects which may have been hidden or dropped as a suspect escapes from the scene of the crime, following tracks by people on the run, chasing and detaining a suspect running away when

they have been challenged to stop, disarming armed suspects and controlling crowds. Because a police dog and handler team can cover very large areas more quick than a single policeman, they are particularly good in a search exercise.

Their ability to scent a human trail from a few hundred yards away and to squeeze into areas where suspects might hide and not be found by a policeman is also a very important part of their success.

General Purpose Dogs are often also trained as Tactical Firearm Support Dogs. They enter a building before the police officer in order to search the building, often with a camera on their heads so their handler can see on a monitor link what or who is in the building. Once the dog has searched and found its target, it must obey the call to return to its handler.

Other skills of the police dogs used by Forces are carried out by Sniffer Dogs – usually Spaniels, German Short Hairs, Labradors or Border Collies. Although these dogs come under different work headings (drugs, explosives, human remains dogs), it is their natural ability to sniff out what they are searching for that puts them under the general heading of sniffer dogs.

They must be driven, but controlled, with a strong temperament and an independent nature. These dogs are trained in different tasks, according to their characters and ability to carry out the job. Sniffer dogs are able to work for a long time without tiring, but their handlers must be aware that they can suffer from nasal fatigue, so need to be rested periodically. They can scent out drugs, either hidden (proactive drug dogs, who search in buildings, cars, etc) or carried on a person (passive drug dogs, working in airports, train stations, concert queues, etc). These dogs also can find cash, explosives, firearms and human remains or blood.

 how2become

Explosives dogs are trained to search, locate and indicate the presence of any type of explosives, no matter how or where they have been made. They work with trained police search teams to search buildings and surrounding areas before visits by Royalty, VIPs and military personnel. Human remains dogs can find bodies or parts of bodies that have been buried or they are able to follow a trail of blood to find where the victim has been hidden.

These dogs are treated as heroes in their own police forces, for the work that they do makes the policemen and women's jobs much easier and enjoyable, when their canine partners are successful in their roles and they can reward them for a job very well done.

CHAPTER 4
POLICE DOG COMMANDS

The first important task to complete when training a police dog is obedience training. Without the total obedience of a dog to its trainer, and subsequently its handler, not only will the task not be carried out, but there could be a danger to the dog, to its handler, to the public, and also to a suspected criminal. Therefore, an intensive programme of training a dog to obey and carry out certain commands is based upon the correct handling of obedience training.

As it is the usual practice to begin training dogs as puppies, trainers can work with each dog according to its character and breed. Obedience is vital in all types of police dog work, although there are commands used according to the type of job required. We will look at the commands themselves after considering the general obedience training.

Above all else the trainer must be consistent in training. Dogs are not human and do not think as humans do, but they learn by repeating exercises that become habitual in response to commands. A dog will not know what a

certain command means without this repetitive command and response, although a trainer must be aware of a dog's capacity to become bored or tired and work beneath this level in all training sessions.

Commands must be repeated clearly, in a level, soft tone and preferably with one word. Some dogs may be quick to pick up on what action is required of them when they hear a command, but some take longer to learn. Each exercise must be understood from each command before a trainer can move on to a new command and exercise. A dog may become confused if it has not understood one command and then is asked to carry out something new. Therefore, training can be quite a long process, but it is important to take each step at the dog's level of understanding.

Obedience training is a progressive programme, with each step being an important part of the whole. The trainer must not only control the dog, but must also control his own temperament and actions, as well as frustrations. The sound and tone of the trainer's voice controls the dog, not the volume of his words. If a soft voice is used, the trainer can encourage the dog to listen more carefully and to concentrate on the command. A command should not be repeated.

The dog must learn to act on a single word. Also, the dog cannot be allowed to ignore a command, even once, as this will instil in it the understanding that it doesn't have to follow a command. If the dog makes a mistake in carrying out a command, this fault must be corrected immediately. The way a dog learns to carry out a task is achieved through this correction and the repetition of the correct way.

Obedience training begins with the dog on a lead. The voice command is accompanied by the physical carrying out of the command with the trainer's guidance. As the dog progresses

in its training, the lead may be taken off and visual prompts or hand signals added. Patience is definitely not only a virtue but a necessity in obedience training.

When a dog is disobedient even though the trainer knows it does understand a command, the trainer needs to be firm with the dog. A dog does not understand right from wrong, but can learn exactly what the trainer is requiring it to do, if the trainer corrects it firmly and patiently. Usually the with-holding of praise is enough to show the dog that its mistake is not accepted. Correction must be appropriate for the type of dog and its temperament, so that the dog is not confused.

The importance of praising the dog's obedience cannot be overstressed. Even if the carrying out of the task was halt-ing or delayed, praise is necessary for the final completion. An obedient dog is a happy dog, and each training session should end with a happy dog and a happy trainer. The rela-tionship is based on an understanding between the pair of command, obedience and praise.

COMMANDS

Heel
With this command, the dog learns to walk on the lead at first on the left side of the trainer with its right shoulder close to the trainer's left knee. The lead should be slack, so as to leave room for the trainer to pull up on the lead to correct the dog. As the trainer holds the lead in his right hand, this leaves his left hand free to give encouragement and praise to the dog.

The dog soon learns that the correct position will make it comfortable and that any discomfort is due to its disobedi-ence to this command. While on the lead, the dog can learn to vary pace and direction according to command.

Once the dog has learned the 'heel' command on the lead, the trainer can move to using the same position without the lead. The trainer should carry the lead so it is visible to the dog but does not impede with the training. The dog then learns to move from 'sit' to 'heel' and back again, in a gradual progression.

Stand

This command is first given when the dog is on 'heel' with the lead. The trainer stops walking, gives the command 'stand' and holds his hand in front of the dog's face. If the dog continues walking or moves in any way, the trainer continues to give the 'stand' command. Once the dog has learned to 'stand', the trainer walks away and leaves the dog in this position. When he returns to the dog, he gives the 'heel' command and they continue to walk.

Sit

Once again, this command is given when the dog is walking on lead with the trainer. He gives the command to 'sit', pulling up on the lead and at the same time pushing down on the dog's rear. When this 'sit' command is understood, the trainer will walk away, leaving the dog sitting. When he returns to the dog, the trainer takes up the lead and begins to walk, commanding the dog to 'heel'. If the dog sits uncomfortably or lopsided, the trainer should correct its posture by pressure with his hand or leg, as the dog sits next to it. The dog will therefore learn to sit in a comfortable position, which will help its alertness to the next command.

Down

The 'down' command is aimed at having the dog assume a prone position instantly, whether the trainer is by the dog's side or at a distance. This command is taught on lead, but should also be practised when the dog is off the lead. In

order to teach the dog what the 'down' command means, the trainer should give the command at the same time as applying gentle downward pressure on the dog's upper back and pulling downwards on a shortened lead.

As soon as the dog is correctly prone, the trainer must immediately take off the pressure. If the dog moves or stands up again, the trainer resumes the downward pressure until the dog is prone once again. When the dog carries out the command by verbal prompt, all physical pressure can discontinue.

Distance control

Once the dog has successfully learned the basic commands of 'heel', 'stand', 'sit' and 'down', the trainer can introduce distance control. This will be necessary in order for the dog to carry out its tasks when the handler cannot be by the dog's side, but requires it to do its job by command.

When the dog has learned the different positions on the lead, the trainer can use an extended lead, which gives the dog the feeling of distance but still keeps it attached to the trainer. The trainer can also move forward while the dog is obeying the commands in the correct position, whether standing, sitting or down. As the dog learns that the trainer's intention is for it to remain in position even when the trainer is not by its side, the trainer can give the commands when the dog is not on lead and the trainer moves forward without the dog.

Usually the distance should be limited to about 15 metres at first, once the trainer has given the command, and then the trainer stops, turns and returns to the dog's left side, turning and coming up again on the dog's right side. When the 'heel' command is given, the dog and trainer both begin to walk again. The distance practice should be done after giving all stationary commands 'stand', 'sit' and 'down'.

 how2become

After the distance factor is clearly understood by the dog commands can then be given from a distance, with the trainer facing the dog in its various stationary postures.

Leaving the dog

This exercise teaches the dog to remain in the 'down' position when the trainer is not physically present. The 'down' command must be fully understood and carried out each time before the trainer can attempt to leave the dog in this position. Progress should be low, to ensure that the dog obeys when the trainer is a short distance away. As the trainer can still see the dog, he can be aware of any movement the dog may make, and if the dog does move out of position, the trainer can return to the dog and ensure it is placed in the correct position before he walks away again.

As the dog progresses in remaining in position during the trainer's distance the trainer can increase the distance until he is actually out of sight of the dog, knowing the dog will remain in position.

During this learning exercise, the trainer should not recall the dog from the 'stay' command, as this would confuse the dog with another command when it has been told to 'stay'.

Recall (or 'Come')

This command is used to bring the dog back to the trainer comfortably and happily, with no reprimand for the dog not carrying out the command. It can first be practised on lead, when the trainer walks in a different direction and calls the dog to his side, at first by pulling on the lead. If the trainer steps backwards or even squats down, the dog may be more encouraged to come. When the dog responds, even tentatively, it should be praised by the trainer. The trainer should never punish the dog for refusing to obey this command, as the dog needs to feel that its return is welcome.

Once the stationary positions are accomplished on command, the trainer can begin training the dog to come from each of the positions. The trainer will need a lot of patience to carry out this training, as it may be a difficult command for the dog to learn. Once the dog can be recalled from all positions, and will 'come' readily to the trainer, then the dog can be taught to be recalled to the 'sit' position. When all this comes together, the dog can then learn to 'heel' from the 'sit' position when the trainer is ready to move on.

Retrieve

This is an important command for any training that follows. Usually a wooden dumbbell is used that is sized for the type and weight of dog. It will have to become familiar to this object in order to feel comfortable in retrieving it. As great concentration is needed for this command to be carried out, the area for training must be free from distractions for the dog.

There are 3 stages of retrieval training:

1. Hold

The trainer begins by encouraging the dog to take hold of the dumbbell with its mouth. If the dog is reluctant to do so, then trainer should apply pressure on the left side of the dog's jaw, while placing the dumbbell in its mouth. When the dog accepts the dumbbell, the trainer pushes slightly on the dog's underjaw in order to impress on it the holding action.

Maintaining a hold on the dumbbell should be connected with the command 'fetch'. Every time the dog learns to take up and hold the dumbbell at this command, the trainer should encourage its obedience by stroking the top of its head.

In order for the dog to release its hold on the dumbbell, the command 'leave' must be taught. Once again, if the dog

does not want to let go of the dumbbell when physically prompted by the trainer trying to take the dumbbell out of its mouth, pressure should be applied on the left side of the dog's jaw in order to teach it to let go. When the trainer receives the dumbbell out of the dog's mouth, praise is given and physical encouragement should be given.

2. Carry

When the dog can 'hold' and 'leave' the dumbbell on command each time, the trainer should begin the task of teaching the dog to 'carry' the dumbbell a distance. This can be done with the dog on lead, in order to allow the trainer to use a gentle pressure on the lead to bring the dog forward as it carries the dumbbell. Should the dog drop the dumbbell, the trainer should replace it in the dog's mouth. The trainer needs to show displeasure by his verbal correction, saying 'hold' to the dog while replacing the dumbbell.

As the trainer backs slowly away and commands the dog to 'come', the dog will learn to carry the dumbbell to the trainer.

3. Delivery

Once the dog understands 'carry' and will bring the dumbbell to the trainer, the trainer should command the dog to sit in front of him and then issue the command to 'leave' the dumbbell. The trainer then removes the dumbbell from the dog's mouth. This should be repeated until the dog will 'fetch', picking up the dumbbell from the ground, 'carry' the dumbbell to a position in front of the trainer and on the command 'leave', allow the trainer to take it from the dog.

When this series of commands is learned, the trainer can then actually throw the dumbbell and, without its lead, the dog can respond to the command to 'fetch' the dumbbell, pick it up and return it to the trainer in a 'sit' position, allowing

him to take the dumbbell from him on the command 'leave'.

Speak

This is a command which can be taught with the dog's natural desire to bark. Police dogs will be asked to 'speak' in circumstances where there is a need to alert of a find, or to keep suspects in place or crowds at bay, or to guard something or someone. It may help to use a prompt in order to ask the dog to 'speak' on cue in order to teach it to respond in the circumstances required.

Send away

This command is needed in order to train the dog to leave the trainer to go in the required direction. It can be difficult to encourage a dog to leave its handler, but patience and perseverance on the trainer's part will succeed.

Again, the training can begin on lead, with the object as a reference point set at a selected position a short distance away that is visible to the dog. The dog starts at a 'stand'

or 'sit' position and the trainer sends the dog to the point of reference, say a coat or toy on the ground. The trainer then moves to the dog and rewards it with praise. Once the dog's confidence is built up in correctly obeying the command, it will also associate the reference point with a happy result. When the dog has learned what it must do, the trainer can repeat the exercise without the lead, increasing the distance to the object gradually.

Eventually, the point of reference becomes invisible to the dog with distance, so the trainer must encourage the dog to keep moving towards the object. This exercise requires the dog's total concentration, so the area of practice needs to be free from distractions and enclosed by a boundary, such as a fence.

Redirection

This command is separate from the 'send away' command, in that it requires the dog to go in a direction the trainer distinguishes to the dog at a distance.

The trainer leaves the dog in a 'sit' or 'stand' position and walks to a half-way point between the dog and the object of reference (point of redirection), which, as above, could be a coat or a toy. The trainer then encourages the dog forward toward the object, keeping him in a straight line (not toward the trainer, but toward the object). As the dog nears the trainer, the trainer should move in a parallel line to the object, all the while encouraging the dog to keep moving toward the object. When the dog reaches the object, the trainer moves to the dog and praises and rewards it.

When both this and the send away commands are mastered successfully, then the trainer can combine the two commands.

Stopping

This is a very important command that brings together all the commands learned earlier by the dog. Training for this usually requires the help of a 'criminal', in order to act out a chase and detain incident. Each dog, according to its inherent drive, will react differently to this exercise. Positive and negative reinforcements are used in this training. The use of a long training line provides the negative reinforcement if a dog will not come to a stop when commanded. The positive reinforcement could be the dog's play toy.

A 'criminal' may emerge from a hiding point nearby and begin to run off, without inciting the dog or appearing to hurry. The trainer tells the 'criminal' to stop and then sends the dog. The trainer throws the dog's toy over its head and commands it to 'stop'. He pulls on the long training lead in order to reinforce his command. The dog is distracted by the toy and when it stops, the trainer gives the dog lots of praise.

This command can be successful only through the work of the earlier obedience training. Once the dog will stop with the long training lead, longer distances can be used to increase the dog's abilities to stop.

Agility

Agility is a natural ability of dogs capable of the rigours of police work. However, agility training must be suited to the type of dog and its own natural limits. Agility is not a command, but it is a necessary requirement for training and can be developed through correct training.

Police dogs must be able to overcome all obstacles within their natural abilities in response to their handlers' commands. The following are training methods used to test and improve a dog's agility through the trainer's commands.

1. Obstacle jump

This training begins with low obstacles that the trainer can easily manage himself, with the dog on lead, carefully ensuring the lead does not tangle or stop the dog in its jump. The dog should be encouraged to approach the centre of the obstacle so it does not try to go around it rather than jumping. The trainer needs to carefully coincide his command with the distance the dog appears to need in order to clear the obstacle, timing this for the dog to begin its jump.

Once the dog understands the command and shows its control of the low obstacles, the height of the obstacles can be increased gradually.

2. Scaling

This command is appropriate for an obstacle which is too high for the dog to jump over, thus requiring it to actually leap up and pull itself over the obstacle. The distance needed for the dog to achieve this is usually the same distance as the obstacle's height.

Although dogs may be capable of scaling very high obstacles, the trainer must remember each particular dog's capabilities and especially its age. Younger dogs should not be pushed beyond their abilities, despite their enthusiasm.

The command control of the trainer is important to keep the dog in check when they reach a great proficiency in scaling obstacles.

3. Long jumping

Training for long jumping involves placing low height obstacles close together and gradually moving them further apart as the dog's abilities increase. This is important in giving the dog the skills to surmount obstacles of gaps, fallen debris, or perhaps ground fires.

4. Water work

Although some dogs take to water well, others need encouragement, as a police dog will inevitably come up against a water obstacle that must be crossed or entered. Training can be started in shallow water, perhaps with the trainer's presence. Gradually the water can get deeper, once the dog is used to walking on the bottom. The trainer can throw objects for the dog to retrieve, increasing the distance and the depth of the water as the dog becomes more proficient in swimming.

CHAPTER 5
POLICE DOG HEALTH CARE

As with any dog it is essential that the correct care is given to the dog both in terms of every day care and health care. This chapter will show you how you should care for your police dog and how to ensure they remain a healthy and happy dog. While in many ways the police dog is just like a normal dog it is also in other ways very different and before you can become a police dog handler you must understand this key concept.

This chapter is broken down into two main sections, the first deals with the general care of your police dog and the second deals with any health problems that may occur and how you can deal with them.

The aim of this chapter is to provide a unique overview of what is required from you as the handler on a daily basis. As the handler you are responsible for the health and safety and day to day care of the dog to enable the dog, and you, to carry out your job in an effective manner. It is your

responsibility to spot potential illnesses and deal with them quickly so that your dog can make a speedy recovery.

Many candidates are simply unaware of what is required of them not only in terms of training the dog but also in terms of caring for the dog. This chapter has also been created to ensure those who want to become police dog handlers are fully aware of what is required from them. Taking on the role of police dog handler is not a 9 to 5 job where you can leave the dog at the police station.

The bond between handler and owner needs to be strong and as a result the dog will live at the handler's house. This means that you will be responsible for your dog 24 hours a day and while this may be difficult at the beginning, while the dog is training, it is significantly easier once they are fully trained. A fully trained police dog is most highly trained dogs in the world the more effort you put into training your police dog the easier the daily care of your dog becomes.

There are 5 key and essential elements to ensure that your police dog is in good physical condition. These include: the daily examination, grooming, high quality food, exercise and quality housing. Each of these elements are discussed in turn throughout this chapter and if you apply each of these on a daily basis you will ensure your dog receives the best possible care. It is important to note that at this point there are other elements that will contribute to the care of your police dog but these are regarded as the top 5 elements.

THE DAILY CARE OF A POLICE DOG

The Daily Health Check

The health of your police dog is vital to your ability to under-take your job when the dog unit is called into action by other sections of the police force. For example, you may be called to the scene of a crime where a car has been stolen and then dumped and the criminal has run off to escape being caught by police officers and your job is to then hunt them down. If your dog is not healthy then he will not be able to function properly and carry out his work to the best of his abilities.

As a result of this it is a good idea to carry out a daily health check of your dog. This does not have to be a long drawn out process but can take you 5 to 10 minutes when you get up or even before you start work.

The first part of the health check is the visual inspection and this will probably take place without you even realising it as it comes naturally to most dog owners. This is a simple visual inspection to check that the dog appears as his normal self:

• Does he greet you in his normal way or is he lying down and not wanting to get up?

• Maybe he is limping?

If you do notice anything out of the ordinary then this should be noted so that you can update the veterinary surgeon at a later date.

Most dog owners will undertake this visual inspection as part of their morning routine but as a police dog handler it becomes a more important process as it could affect the dog's daily work and potentially put them and you in danger if called into action. As a police dog handler you will spend a lot of time with your dog and as a result irregularities are often quickly discovered.

The second part of the daily health check is not something that most dog owners would undertake on a daily basis, but is something that you will need to as a police dog handler. The second part is carrying out a physical examination on your dog with the aim of checking the whole of your dog's body to discover any potential lumps or injuries. This involves checking the ears, eyes, nose, mouth, legs, feet and genitals.

With regards to the ear you will want to look out for any redness or swelling of the ear, any discharge from the ear, excessive wax production or any indication from the dog that there is pain in one ear. Where the dog scratches its ear, shakes his head frequently, carries the ear down this can also indicate a problem with the ear. If cleaning is necessary the ears may be gently wiped with cloth dipped in warm soapy water.

For the eyes as an owner you should look out for any discharge or change in colour. In terms of your dog's nose it should be cold and wet and a dry nose could indicate a high temperature (although this could be the result of a training session in a hot weather). When checking the mouth you should check to ensure there are no broken teeth, the gums are looking healthy and the dog's breath is not different from normal (as this can indicate a stomach upset).

For your dog's legs and feet you will need to check for lumps or cysts, make sure they are free from objects such as thorns or twigs. In addition to this tar can sometimes collect on the hair between the pads and can cause eczema if it is not removed. A key point to note is that a dog that receives regular exercise will generally keep its feet in good order and regular walking on solid ground such as pavements will keep their nails trim.

The dog has two anal glands, one at each side of the anus, approximately at the 4 and 8 o'clock positions. These are modified skin glands which produce a secretion. The glands are rather liable to become blocked, particularly in G.S.D.s, probably because of the down-pressed tail carriage. When this occurs there is quite a lot of irritation produced and dog will rub its bottom on the ground, suddenly sit down and start up again quickly, look round at its tail or lick and bite at the tail root. If the condition is not relieved abscess formation may occur.

GROOMING

Grooming your police dog on a regular basis is one of the five elements to keep your dog in a good condition. It is also a mark of the trainer and shows the sense of pride they have in their dog. Police dog handlers will often pride themselves on the appearance of their police dogs but this is not the main or a significant reason why grooming should be part of your daily routine.

Apart from cleaning the coat and skin, regular grooming helps to keep both in a good healthy condition by removing any dead skin or hair and therefore helps prevent the build up of parasites. In addition to this grooming helps to develop and build a stronger level of trust between handler and dog.

Grooming is an activity that can and should be built into part of your daily routine as a dog handler and many handlers will use this as an opportunity to carry out the daily health check (which has been described above). For example, while you are grooming your police dog you can take this opportunity to check for any wounds or possible injuries.

Key Tools Used For Grooming:

1. Your Hands

2. A Brush

3. A Comb

The 3 steps for correctly grooming your police dog:

1. Use your hands to massage the dog's coat and this will stimulate circulation within the dog's skin.

2. Use the brush to firstly brush the coat following the direction of the hair and then against the direction of the hair.

3. Use the comb as the final step in the process to tidy up the coat and ensure all dead skin / hair has been removed.

By massaging your dog's skin you will stimulate blood to this area and help maintain a glossy coat. However, some dog handlers will use materials such as leather or silk to polish the dog's coat and to increase the shine of the coat. This is not a necessary step for effective grooming and is an individual choice that can be taken by the owner.

When you have completed the grooming process you will need to ensure that the combs and brushes are cleaned before putting them away. A comb or brush that is not clean will struggle to get the desired results next time around. If you are handling more than one police dog you will need to keep separate grooming materials for each dog. Once you have cleaned your grooming tools it is always a good idea to wash your own hands as a matter of personal hygiene.

FEEDING

Another key element in the care of your police dog is ensuring

the dog receives the correct food at the correct times. Many dogs that are kept as pets eat at regular times throughout the day and this is no exception for the police dog. Creating a sense of regularity at meals times is essential to training a successful police dog as you will both be required to work certain hours.

In similar ways to that of a human, a police dog needs a balanced diet to ensure that they receive the necessary nutrients and minerals to complete and recover from their daily tasks. A balanced diet is even more important for a police dog as it will provide essential energy to enable them to perform all the training tasks and duties expected of a police dog on a daily basis.

The police dog needs to receive the right amount of water, fats, protein, vitamins and carbohydrates to ensure that they achieve this balance. A sufficient supply of water is also an essential part of keeping your dog healthy and hydrated and you should always try to ensure that there is always a bowl of fresh water.

THE TIME TO FEED YOUR DOG

Generally adult dogs are fed once a day and to avoid any disturbance of the digestive system they should, if possible, be fed at the same time each day. Younger dogs or puppies may require feeding on a more regular basis maybe two or three times a day with smaller meals as they are still growing. There is no set or recommend time to feed dog and it will be down to the individual handler when this takes place and they will often take into consideration their work commitments.

The key point to remember is to try and choose a convenient

time that you will be able to stick to each day so that you create consistent feeding pattern. If a dog is fed at different times each day this will not only off set their digestive system but will also affect their ability to function and perform. Another point to bear in mind is that it is not advisable to feed your dog immediately before or after work or exercise. Give them enough time to recover from their activities before feeding.

THE FEED

To ensure your police dog receives a complete and balanced diet there are two main options available to you and your choice of option will typically depend upon the amount of time you can dedicate to preparing meals, the cost, and availability. The first option is to prepare a fresh diet of meat and vegetables which will require you to take time to prepare this meal each evening, and the second more modern option is to use prepared dog food. The second option is often selected as the choice of convenience especially for those owners that have more than one dog.

While this option is the healthier option there are a number of factors you need to consider. Firstly you will need to give some consideration to each meal to ensure that the protein and fat content of each piece of meat provides the correct balance. The piece of meat will also need to be cooked well to ensure that all bacteria is removed but not too much that it loses its nutritional value. If you prepare a piece of fish care must be taken to remove all bones before it is fed to the dog.

With regards to vegetables it is preferable that these be steamed to reduce the loss of nutrients and not all dogs will take to all vegetables. It may take some trial and error to determine which vegetables your dog will eat. While

selecting this option is a healthier way to prepare the meals for your dog it will typically be a more expensive option than already prepared dog food. However, it is an option that can easily be incorporated into your daily routine as you can pre-pare these meals at the same time as you prepare your own.

The second option and the option taken by the majority of dog handlers and dog owners is to buy prepared dog food which is seen as being the more convenient and time saving option. However, there are now a number of pre-prepared dog foods that offer a complete all in one meal which have been specifically designed to ensure they have the correct amount of protein, carbohydrates, vitamins and nutrients to form a balanced diet.

Within the pre-prepared option there are canned dog food, dry dog food and semi-moist dog food. Canned dog food will provide all the nutrients required although they will usu-ally require the addition of dried biscuits to provide sufficient energy for the dog. Dry dog food will normally have a higher level of nutrients than canned foods and include a greater level of carbohydrates to the point where additional supple-ments to the meal are not required. While they all have their own benefits it is up to the individual handler which type of food they choose and the key point to remember is to try and achieve a balanced diet.

AFTER THE FEED

Once the feeding has taken place always allow your dog time to relieve themselves and never shut a dog away straight after eating a meal otherwise you may return to unpleasant consequences. All feeding equipment should be thoroughly washed after use and the dog should be given a reasonable time to consume their food. If after this time there is still

food left over then it should be disposed of and not left in their bowl. It is also recommended to allow your dog time to relieve themselves after their feed and if you can build this into part of their daily routine it will make your life as the trainer a lot easier.

EXERCISE

A significant part of creating a balanced and healthy dog is to ensure that the dog receives enough exercise. This is not only true of dogs kept as pets but also for police dogs. While a police dog will often have a training regime during the working day which involves a great deal of exercise, it is also important to ensure the dog receives exercise outside of the working environment. This will ideally be first thing in the morning or last thing at night and means that the dog does not only associate exercise with work. It will also help develop a stronger bond and increase the level of trust between the police dog and handler.

HOUSING

The final key element to ensuring that your police dog receives a balanced and healthy life is through appropriate housing. Police Dogs are often kept in a kennel at the home of the handler. This is another consideration to bear in mind where applying for the position of a police dog handler. Does your house have enough space to support a kennel and maintain a dog? Whereas dogs that are kept as pets may remain inside the house during the night the police dog is trained to sleep within a kennel.

Kennels usually take two forms; they are either permanent or temporary and must meet certain standards to be

considered acceptable. It is recommended that the kennel at the handler's house should be a temporary structure in case it needs to be removed, whereas the kennel at the training centre is often a permanent structure.

As a police dog handler a kennel is important to maintaining the health of your police dog and as a result you need to make sure that it is secure and waterproof and that the dog has enough room to stand up. It is also recommend that the kennel is raised off of the ground to prevent the formation of damp, which could lead to the development of rheumatism

Location is also an important consideration when placing a kennel at the home of the handler. An ideal location would be a quiet one where the dog can receive adequate light, there is space outside the kennel to move around and protected from strong winds. The provision of additional bedding in the kennel may be required during the winter months when it is considerably colder at night.

If the kennel fails to match up to the basic standards described above then your dog could quickly become unwell and this will affect their ability to perform their job.

MAINTAINING THE KENNEL

The kennel should be cleaned on a daily basis with any excrement removed from the kennel and disposed of in the appropriate manner. If this has happened then it is recommend that the kennel be correctly disinfected and allowed to completely dry before allowing the dog to return into the kennel. As mentioned previously if the kennel remains wet then this can lead to the build up of damp.

KENNEL EQUIPMENT REQUIRED

- A feeding bowl
- A water bowl
- A shovel
- A type of disinfectant
- Additional bedding for use during the winter

BATHING

Bathing your dog is not included as one of the essential elements for the reason that provided the daily grooming is properly carried out bathing is not necessarily required. In fact regular bathing can have the opposite effect and can make the dog appear unhealthy by removing the natural grease from the dogs coat and skin which in turn reduces the shine.

If you feel that it is necessary to bath your dog, for example, they may be covered in mud that cannot easily be removed through grooming, then be sure you use warm water with proper dog shampoo. Always ensure that the shampoo is thoroughly removed and that the dog is completely dry before letting them back outside.

The last ten years has also seen a massive growth in dog grooming industry and there are now various dog grooming companies that can provide this service for you. In more recent years there has been a rapid growth in mobile dog grooming companies who will come to your house and carry out a wide range of dog grooming services on your dog.

As well as bathing your dog they will also be able to offer trimming services to remove long hair, cut back nails and

removing hair balls to name just a few. However, these are all things that can be carried out by the handler.

There are many ways to find one of these companies and the quickest is to simply search the internet for the phrase "dog grooming" in your local area. Alternatively, a directory such as the yellow pages will also provide similar results. While this may be the quicker and more convenient option you will have to consider the cost of this and once again this will be a choice for the individual owner.

POLICE DOG HEALTH CARE

One of the core elements is the daily health check and the reason a handler must do this on a regular basis is to enable early diagnosis of any illnesses. By understanding the signs and symptoms you will be able to detect a disease or illness much earlier and this could save your dog's life. If you do notice anything wrong with your dog you should always write the information down so that it can easily be relayed to the vet at a later date.

Within this section we will go through the common types of symptoms that you dog may experience, how you can look out for them as the handler and what steps you should take. The aim is to make you feel confident about looking after your dog by providing you with everything you need to know.

If at any point during your dog's training or even their life you are unsure about a particular symptom or illness always consult your vet for expert advice. As a handler you must not assume the role of the vet and carry out diagnosis yourself, best to leave this to the professionals.

As the dog is unable to speak to inform you that they do not feel well or what their symptoms are it is up to you as the

handler to recognise the early warning signs. Early recognition will often result in early treatment of a disease which will aid a speedy recovery. A sign or symptom of a disease or illness should never be ignored in the hope that it will disappear and this could prove to be a fatal mistake.

The behaviour of each police dog will differ from the next police dog and so it is up to the handler to determine when the dog's behaviour is out of the ordinary. For example, what might be normal behaviour for one dog may not be normal behaviour for another. This type of information should always be passed on to a kennel assistant especially if they are looking after more than one police dog at the same time.

As a general rule it is always a good idea to keep a check on the frequency, colour and consistency of the bowel movements of each dog. Any irregularities in these from normal patterns can often be an early sign or symptom that your dog is unwell or suffering from a disease.

TYPICAL SYMPTOMS

The following are a list of symptoms that your dog may experience and as the handler you must watch out for them:

Your Dog Looses Their Appetite

What this means: A loss of appetite can be an indication of a number of factors and can vary from an upset stomach, tired from being over trained or an early indication of a more serious disease. If this loss of appetite has been going on for a little while then it is recommended that you take your dog to the vet for further advice. If this is the first time you have noticed this and you know the dog has had a hard training session then it is down to you if you wait to see if their appetite returns to the dog the next day or take them to the vet straight away.

Excessive Appetite

What this means: This will typically depend upon the age of your dog. If you are raising a puppy or have younger dogs they will generally have an excessive appetite as they are still growing and this is quite normal. However, if your dog is an adult dog and has an excessive appetite and is constantly demanding more food then this could indicate the presence of worms or even a more serious condition such as diabetes.

KEY POINTS

With regards to the health of your dog there are generally two types of worms you need to be looking out for. One is often found in the puppy and this is called round worm, whereas tapeworm is usually found in adult dogs. Worms will often only be visible in the faeces or in the dog vomit. Puppies should be wormed at 14, 21, 28 and then 60 days old and then every year thereafter. Tape worms found in adult dogs are not as easy to eradicate and if you discover your dog has thus type of worm, you should seek veterinary advice for the best way to eradicate this problem.

Bad Breath

What this means: Dog's typically have bad breath and this should not alarm you if you suddenly discover this about your dog. However, the more you work with your dog the more you will come to recognise what your dog's breath is like. It is any changes from this regular smell that you should look out for as a dog owner. Changes in your dog's breath could indicate changes in their stomach such as an upset stomach.

However, bad breath in dogs is usually a result of dental problems such as a build up of tartar. The build up of tartar can be prevented by providing your dog with dental chews

or treats. For more serious problems such as a reddening of the gums you should consult your registered vet.

Rapid or sharp Breathing

What this means: Once again you must consider the circumstances by which the dog is experiencing sharp or rapid breathing. For example, if you have just undertaken an intensive training session then your dog may experience rapid breathing and this is normal. However, if your dog is lying down and has not been active for a while and you notice their rapid or sharp breathing this should be a cause for concern. It can be an indication of an issue or problem with the lungs or chest area such as bronchitis or pneumonia. You should then seek immediate consultation from a vet.

Constipation

There are several possible reasons for constipation. Diet appears to play a significant role and a prolonged lack of exercise, a change in surroundings, or a change in daily routine (e.g. stress) can lead to constipation problems as well.

Constipation is less common in police dogs than in other dogs for the simple reason that police dogs undertake a lot more and regular exercise and it is often a lack of exercise that can result in constipation. For example, a dog that is kept as a pet may be locked away or confined to a small area until the owner returns from work. The amount of exercise they receive can then be restricted to one or two hours a day. On the other hand a police dog will be active on a regular basis throughout the day during their training or as part of their work.

There are a number of simple methods which you can employ to increase the bowl activity of your dog and relieve any constipation. Increasing the exercise that your dog gets

will help with their bowl movement, and by grooming your dog on a regular basis this will reduce the hair build up in the stomach. Herbal remedies such as laxatives may also help to relieve the dog in the short term however this may not solve the problem.

You should also review the diet your dog is on and see if there are any changes that can be made. For example, also ensure there is fresh water available; increase the fibre in their diet and an excess amount of biscuits or bones should be avoided. Your vet will be able to advise you which steps are best suited to your dog.

Cough

If your dog has a cough it could indicate a number of health problems, for example a throat or chest infection or some-thing more serious such as hard pad or distemper. In an age-ing dog this could also be a sign of heart disease.

Diarrhoea:

Diarrhoea occurs when food travels through the digestive system too quickly, resulting in insufficient moisture being absorbed. Diarrhoea is often due to stress, such as new envi-ronment, over-training, change of diet, eating spicy foods, medications and stress. As you can see there are a number of possible causes for diarrhoea and whatever the cause, the aim of is to give the intestines a rest and a chance to recover.

This is usually done under instruction from the vet by removing food for 24 hours. After this 24 hour period the vet will typically specify a diet to follow for the next few days. However, if symptoms persist then return to your vet for further advice. You should also bear in mind that diar-rhoea in puppies should be monitored more carefully as it has the potential to be life threatening if left untreated.

Discharge from the Eyes

What this means: a watery discharge in both eyes turning to mucus and matter is present in distemper and, to a lesser degree, in hard pad. A similar condition may be seen in dogs which have been exposed to draughts, e.g. having their heads out of car windows. Inflammation in one eye may be due to injury or a foreign-body such as a grass seed. Occasionally one sees a grey opaque condition of the transparent part of the eye, with no accompanying discharge, and this may be due to viral hepatitis.

Texture of the Nose changes

What this means: a dog's nose is normally cool and moist due to the evaporation of liquid produced by special glands in the skin of the area. In some diseases, particularly where there is a high temperature, the nose feels hot and dry, but this is by no means constant and it should only be regarded as a possible pointer to ill-health. In distemper and hard pad, the nose becomes caked with discharge and cracked, and in the latter disease one may see hardening and thickening of the skin of the nose.

Increased temperature

What this means: the normal rectal temperature of the dog is 101.5F. The temperature is raised in infectious diseases, in painful conditions, or even when the dog is excited or nervous. The rectal temperature is a very important guide to the dog's condition and should be one of the first points to be checked when illness is suspected. If the dog is excited or nervous at the time of examination, re-check the temperature after a period of rest in a quiet kennel. The temperature may also fall below normal in some hormone deficiencies such as a sluggish thyroid gland, in circulatory collapse, e.g. shock.

Becoming Thirsty

What this means: thirst is increased in various conditions. A high salt content of the diet, hot weather, vomiting and diarrhoea can all lead to an excessive water intake. Chronic kidney disease, heart disease and diabetes are serious diseases which are signalled by increased thirst.

Changes to the dog's Urine:

What this means: variation in the frequency or urination, the amount and character of the urine passed are all important pointers to disease.

Vomiting

What this means: any condition which irritates the stomach may cause vomiting. For this reason, the occasional vomiting attack should not be regarded too seriously, but if vomiting persists, or if frequent, then veterinary advice should be obtained as soon as possible. Vomiting may be seen in infectious diseases such as distemper, bowel obstruction, inflammation of stomach and bowels, and liver disease.

COMMON ILLNESSES OR DISEASES

- **Rabies** - A virus present in the saliva of an affected animal, the virus passes along the nerves and reaches the central nervous system causing paralysis and eventually death. Rabies is always fatal and is often indicated through excessive salivation and foaming at the mouth, followed by paralysis.

- **Fleas** - Fleas coming into contact with humans in an environment where cat and dog fleas are breeding. Fleas bite and cause irritation of the skin. To prevent fleas the dog should be given Anti-flea treatment on a regular basis.

- **Roundworm -** Mature worms inhabiting the canine intestine lay eggs which are passed in the faeces of the dog. The eggs, which are sticky, adhere to hands, clothes, etc. and are ingested by humans. Eggs hatch in the body and migrate to varying parts of the body. This can be prevented by maintaining a high level of cleanliness especially after you have come into contact with your dog.

- **Weil's disease –** This caused by an organism in the urine of an infected animal, usually a rat. It causes loss of appetite, depression, marked thirst, vomiting and loss of weight in your dog. It can lead to coma and eventually death but it can be prevented by regular vaccination.

- **Scabies -** The transfer of the mange mite from an infected dog. The result is that the mite burrows below the skin on hands, wrists and causes an irritating rash. Early diagnosis of any skin condition is the best form of treatment in this case and highlights the importance of the daily health check.

- **Tetanus (Lock Jaw) -** This is a specific disease of domesticated animals and man caused by an organism which obtains access to the tissues through a wound. The organism is present in most cultivated soils and the dog can carry the organism which can only enter the body through an open wound. The organism thrives only in an absence of oxygen, which means it would in fact be better wound heal from the inside out.

  In humans 'lock jaw' occurs which means a stiffness of the joints and jaws. In the dog the owner may notice something peculiar about the eyes and mouth, and

stiffness of limbs is noticeable. Despite treatment, only few animals fully recover from tetanus. The best form of protection is from vaccination.

- **ZOONOSIS** - is the term applied to diseases which are transmissible from animals to humans. Most domestic animals, including dogs, cats, birds, horses and rabbits are capable of transmitting some disease, but the risk is minimal if simple hygienic precautions are taken. For example, always ensure that you wash your hands after contact with your dog.

KEY POINTS ON INOCULATIONS

- Vaccines are now available which will protect against all the common infections of the dog, e.g. distemper, hard pad, viral hepatitis, leptospiral jaundice, parvovirus and leptospiral nephritis.

- The vaccine is given in two doses at a fortnightly interval, preferably when the puppy is 10-12 weeks old.

- The leptospiral fraction of the vaccine must be repeated annually and it is recommended that the virus vaccine should be boosted by a further dose at 2 years of age.

- The parvovirus vaccine should be repeated annually.

KEY POINTS ON VETERINARY RECORDS

- Comprehensive veterinary records for all police dogs which provide a detailed account of their medical history.

- Veterinary Records should be readily available for inspection at all times.

- They should contain details of diagnosis and treatment,

details of the dog's weight which should be recorded weekly; worming tablets issued and include a record of inoculations.

CHAPTER 6
BECOMING A POLICE OFFICER

THE POLICE OFFICER

The great thing about the life of a Police Officer is that you have the ability to make a difference. On many occasions you will be able to change people's lives by the actions you take. It is a demanding but highly satisfying career, and will provide you with the opportunity to make a difference to your community. You will be challenged daily but will have the tools and skills to be confident in your own ability to do the right thing.

Working in the Police Service is a challenging job with many rewards. It provides the opportunity to perform a wide range of roles and to take personal responsibility for helping others. The service strives to treat everyone fairly and you should also be prepared to do the same. Dignity and respect are key elements of a Police Officer's working life.

There is no greater feeling than bringing offenders to justice,

especially if it has involved hard work, gathering information, intelligence, identifying the offender and making the arrest. Unfortunately, for every offender there will be at least one victim and the arrest means nothing if justice in a court does not follow. When all these aspects come together you know then that you've joined a very special team.

Police Officers are responsible for maintaining law and order, and providing a service to the public that ensures their safety, well being and the security of their property and possessions. Above all, they are there to serve the community and this principle is the basis of all policing policy in the UK. It is important that you remember that you are there to serve the public and you don't think that life as a Police Officer is all about catching and convicting criminals.

You must be prepared to have the community's interests at heart. Duties can include patrolling on foot or in cars, investigating crime scenes or attending incidents and interacting with your community. Of course, there will be times when you need to work on the administrative side of the role, and also you will need to be prepared to spend time in court giving evidence. It is a demanding and responsible job.

The rewards are that you can help prevent crime and protect the public, but policing can also be frequently emotionally taxing and challenging. You need to ensure that you are prepared for this side of the job. You might be called on to tell a mother that her daughter has been injured or killed in a road accident, or endure verbal abuse while investigating an incident.

It can also be physically gruelling, for example you might spend seven hours on the beat in extremely cold conditions. More than 35,000 people apply to join the police each and every year so the competition is fierce. Only 5,000 of those

applicants are usually successful so it is vital that you pre-pare yourself well in advance of the application process. By investing in this guide we believe that you are taking positive steps to increase your chances of success.

The most common reason that the UK Police Force turn people down is due to their lack of physical fitness. In total there are 43 police forces and more than 126,000 police officers in England and Wales - about one for every 400 people. In Scotland there are eight police forces. The person in charge of each force is a Chief Constable, except in London, where the Metropolitan Police and the City of London Police are each headed by a Commissioner.

POLICE PROBATIONER TRAINING

After the initial recruitment stage, you'll undergo an intensive training programme as a probationer constable. The first section of this training period usually lasts about 30 weeks and you'll spend some of this time learning core policing skills at a training centre.

The remainder of your time will be spent on patrol with a tutor constable gaining practical operational experience. Gradually you'll take on more tasks on your own until you are ready for independent patrol. This type of on-the-job training will give you the opportunity to practise your newly acquired skills under supervision in a relatively safe environment. But your training doesn't end there. You will receive further training during the remainder of your probation and your performance will be continually assessed.

Then, at the end of the 2 year probationary period, you will hopefully be offered a full contract of employment. The probationary period is an opportunity for you to continually

develop and prove that you have what it takes to become a competent Police Officer.

THE INITIAL POLICE TRAINING COURSE (STAGES)

The two-year probationer training programme is made up of a number of key stages which are identified below:

Stage 1 - Introduction to policing
Gain a basic understanding of the role of a police officer. Learn how to deliver the best service to the public. Some forces extend this to up to five weeks and include elements (like a driving course) that most other forces cover in Stage 6.

Stage 2 - Training Centre, 12 - 15 weeks
Here you'll study the law and learn the core skills you'll need to deal effectively and professionally with a range of operational incidents. Your ANNUAL LEAVE is usually taken on your successful completion of stage 2. This will be an ideal time to re-charge your batteries and prepare for the next stages of your training period.

Stage 3 - Usually 2 weeks
Be prepared for accompanied patrol. Learn about local procedures, force priorities and the communities you will serve/ that you will be serving in.

Stage 4 - On patrol with a Tutor, 10 weeks
Work with a trained tutor constable as you put everything you have learned into practice on patrol under his or her guidance.

Stage 5 - 2 weeks
Your suitability for independent patrol will be assessed and it

is time to think about your further development. Learn more about local procedures and local policing plans. If you're not quite ready for independent patrol at the 31-week stage, you'll receive further tutoring.

Stage 6 - Remainder of probation and training

Complete the rest of your probation on Division, with a minimum of 30 days dedicated to further training. This final stage ensures you are conducting core operational tasks in accordance with good practice. Your performance will be assessed in terms of competence, skills and knowledge.

METROPOLITAN POLICE SERVICE (MPS) PROBATIONER TRAINING

Stage 1 - Residential at Hendon, 18 weeks

You will receive a general introduction to policing where you'll gain a basic understanding of the role of a police officer (with specific focus on policing within

London). You'll learn all the core policing skills and knowledge needed to deal effectively with a range of operational incidents.

Stage 2 - Street Duties Course, 10 weeks

You will be posted to a London borough, where you'll work with a trained tutor constable. He or she will then teach you about local procedures and help you to put everything you have learned into practice. At the end of this stage you'll move on to independent patrol where you'll be able to use your skills on your own.

Stage 3 - Remainder of probation including a further 30 days' minimum training

THE POLICE PENSIONS SCHEME

As a police officer you will automatically join the Police Pension Scheme. This is not mandatory although it is not common for people to opt out of the scheme. If you choose not to join the Police pension scheme then you can choose to make your own pension arrangements.

The Police Pension scheme contribution rate is currently 11% of your pensionable pay. Pension contributions made during previous employment may be transferred to the Police Pension Scheme. For example you may have been employed within the Armed Forces and wish to transfer your pension over to the Police scheme.

You must, however, be aware that you may not receive equal transfer years as most other schemes do not equate to the same time period in the Police Force.

THE WORKING WEEK

A normal working week for a Police Officer consists of 40 hours, which is usually divided up on a shift basis. The shift pattern that you will normally work will form part of your contract and these do vary between each Police Force. All of the ranks below superintendent will be given two rest days every week and compensation will be given if you ever have to work during those two days. If you need to know more about the different types of shift patterns then we recommend you contact your local constabulary.

CHANGING CAREERS

Many people these days change careers during the course of their working lives for various reasons, whether they are

bored with their own job or just fancy a change.

The police force does recognise that people's experience in other careers can be an advantage. An ability to communicate and interact with other members of the community is an essential skill that UK Police Forces are looking for. If you have worked in a customer service roll or delivered a service to customers, you may have the skills that they need.

Examples include shop workers or people who have worked in a caring environment; in fact the list is endless so don't rule yourself out if you are already working and want a new fresh challenge. The Police Force also welcome women who are returning back to work after a break.

MATERNITY LEAVE AND CAREER BREAKS

Women Police Officers are entitled to take a period of maternity leave. You are entitled to take maternity leave from six months before your expected birth date and also for nine months after the expected birth date. You do not have to use all of this period but are entitled to take part of it if you so wish.

All women Police Officers have the right to go back to work following their period of maternity leave, which is good news for those people who choose to start a family. You will also find that the Police Force support those who wish to work on a 'reduced hours' basis, whether that be part time or job sharing.

Officers are entitled to five days' paid maternity support leave if they are the child's father, the partner or the nominated carer of an expectant mother at the time of birth. Adoptive parents are allowed to take five days paid adoption leave at or around the expected time of adoption.

Police Officers who have completed their probationary period are also allowed to apply for a career break up to a maximum of five years. The terms of the career break will form part of an agreed contract between yourself and your respective Police Service. Acceptance onto the career break scheme will be at the discretion of the relevant Chief Constable.

CRIME AND DISORDER REDUCTION PARTNERSHIPS

Crime is tackled in every local area by Crime & Disorder Reduction Partnerships

(CDRPs) – A combination of police, local authorities and other organisations and businesses who have banded together to develop and implement strategies for tackling crime and disorder at the local level.

There are 376 CDRPs to cover nearly every local authority area in England and Wales. Each one produces an audit and strategy for its local area. Many CDRP groups look into community issues relating to their own particular area and some of those issues are concerned with the reduction of crime, antisocial behaviour, graffiti and fly-tipping to name but a few.

It is far easier for Local Authorities (Councils) to improve community safety when they work in collaboration with other stakeholders such as the Fire and Rescue Service, Social Services, The Probation Service, CCTV working groups etc. For many years Police Forces and other stakeholders worked in isolation until it was identified that more could be done if they worked with other relevant partners.

It is important to be aware that your work as a Police Officer may be as a direct result of requests from CDRP groups. For

example there may be a problem with anti-social behaviour in a specific area of your County and you will be working hard to combat the problem.

POLICE COMMUNITY SUPPORT OFFICERS (PCSOS)

Police Community Support Officers do not have the same powers as a fully-fledged police officer, yet they are a highly important part of the crime prevention tool.

They carry out visible patrolling within a specific area and are an effective crime deterrent, especially with regard to anti-social behaviour. Members of the public are more likely to provide PCSOs with important information relating to crime and anti-social behaviour as they spend more time in a specific area getting to know the Community.

As well as being able to issue fixed penalty tickets for minor anti-social behaviour, PCSOs can also demand the name and address of a person acting in an antisocial manner. This information can then be passed on to the Police so that the relevant action can be taken.

Other PCSO powers include being able to confiscate alcohol being consumed in a public place, confiscate tobacco from young people who are under age and seize any vehicles that are being used to potentially harm other people such as by joy-riders.

CRITERIA FOR JOINING THE POLICE

Age
Applications can be accepted at the age of 18 for appointment at 18½. The good news is that there is no upper age limit for applying to the police service. Most people believe

that you have to be below 30 to join but there are many cases of people joining the police force well above this age. You should remember, however, that the normal retirement age for a Police Officer is 55 years old and you will need to carry out a 2 year probation period. Candidates who have reached the age of 18 years may apply to become a police officer and can take up appointment on reaching the age of 18½.

Height

There are no minimum or maximum height requirements to join the police force. Again most people believe that you need to be a certain height to become a Police Officer but as described this is no longer true. Don't worry what height you are as everyone has something to offer whether they are 4 foot tall or 7 foot tall. It is your abilities that count!

Driving Qualifications

The good news is that you will not be rejected if you cannot drive. The requirement to drive does not form part of the criteria for becoming a Police Officer.

Entry Qualification Requirements

There are no formal educational requirements for recruitment to the police service. However, applicants will need to sit 2 written tests to ensure that they have a suitable level of English. There will also be a test of a candidate's numeric ability.

Business Interests

Under normal circumstances you will not be permitted to hold any of the following business interests:

- You hold any office or employment for hire or gain (other than as a police officer) or you carry on any type of business.

- Your spouse or any other relative living with you keeps a shop or similar in the area of the police force that you are applying to join.

- You, your spouse or any relative living with you holds or has a financial interest in any licence or permit relating to liquor licensing, refreshment houses or betting and gaming, or the regulation of places of entertainment in the area of the police force that you are attempting to join.

However, if any of the above criteria apply to you then it is still worth applying as the relevant Chief Police Officer may deem that there is no conflict of interest.

Fitness

To demonstrate a suitable level of fitness you have to undertake a fitness test.

The Police fitness test is not difficult but there are normally 3 different elements to the test and you must pass all of them before you can be appointed as a Police Officer.

The Police are basically looking for a minimum standard that will enable to enable you to carry out your role as a police officer. You will be given help to improve your fitness and if you prepare yourself properly, there is no reason for you to fail.

If you don't pass the test at your first attempt you will be allowed to retake it at a later stage, but if you fail to pass the test after 3 attempts you will not be eligible to apply for another 6 months so make sure you work hard at the first attempt. There are 2 elements to the test: dynamic strength and endurance fitness. Please see our separate section on the fitness test for further information.

Tattoos

Before you apply to join the Police you should check whether the tattoos you have (if any) may cause offence. The UK Police Force has the following criteria in relation to tattoos:

Tattoos are not acceptable if they:

- Undermine the dignity and authority of the office of the constable;

- Are garish or numerous or particularly prominent;

- Could cause offence to members of the public or colleagues and/or invite provocation. This would include tattoos that are rude, lewd, crude, racist, sexist, sectarian, homophobic, violent or intimidating, or tattoos that display unacceptable attitudes towards women, minority groups or any other section of the community, or alignment with particular groups that could cause offence to members of the community.

Your Financial Status

Applicants will have their financial status checked. These checks are carried out because police officers have access to privileged information, which may make them vulnerable to corruption.

It is important that applicants are not under pressure from unpaid debts or liabilities. This does not mean that sensible management of debts or loans, such as a mortgage, will preclude you. Applicants who have existing County Court Judgements outstanding against them will be rejected.

Applicants who have discharged County Court Judgements will be considered. Applicants who have been registered bankrupt and their bankruptcy debts have not been discharged will be rejected. Applicants who have been

registered as bankrupt and their bankruptcy debts have been discharged will not be considered until three years after the discharge of the debt.

If you have discharged bankruptcy debts then you will need to provide a 'Certificate of Satisfaction' with your application. If you are unsure of your financial status then we advise that you check your financial status with an independent body. This can be done usually at little cost, in confidence and online.

Criminal Convictions

Police officers must respect and uphold the law. They should be law-abiding and have a high standard of behaviour and social conduct. Officers with criminal associations or convictions may be vulnerable to pressure to disclose information.

Convictions and cautions for certain offences can also undermine a police officer's position as a witness in court. For these reasons, police forces need to be careful about recruiting people with cautions or convictions.

Although you may still be eligible to join the police service if you have minor convictions/cautions, there are certain offences and conditions that will make you ineligible. Read the following and if you are still unsure, contact your local recruitment office:

- Burglary and offences that involve elements or acts of dishonesty, corruption, substantial financial gain or serious loss to anyone including theft, fraud and deception. Serious involvement in drugs including possession of a Class A drug (heroin, morphine) or more than one Class B drug (amphetamines) and/or supplying drugs of any kind

- Reckless or dangerous driving; or one offence of drink-driving, drunk in charge, or drugs driving, within the last

ten years. Other serious motoring offences such as convictions within the last five years, driving without insurance, failing to stop after an accident or driving whilst disqualified.

- More than three endorsable traffic convictions (including fixed penalties) and/or two or more convictions for regulatory offences within the last five years such as failure to renew a vehicle excise licence.

AS WITH ALL ADVICE CONTAINED WITHIN THIS GUIDE PLEASE CHECK WITH YOUR LOCAL RECRUITMENT OFFICE FIRST FOR YOUR ELIGIBILITY IF UNSURE.

Criminal Conviction - Exclusions

Applications will not be accepted from those who have been convicted or cautioned for a serious arrestable offence including:

- Murder;
- Manslaughter;
- Death by reckless driving;
- Rape;

- Kidnapping;
- Firearms offences;
- Hostage taking;
- Hijacking or torture.

In general, applications will also be rejected if an applicant has:

- Committed any offence (as an adult or juvenile) that resulted in a prison sentence, including custodial, suspended or deferred sentence and sentences served at a young offenders' institution or community home.

- Received a formal caution (including reprimands and final warnings) for a recordable offence within the last five years.

- Been convicted as a juvenile within the last five years for any recordable offence.

- Any other recordable offence within the last five years other than those listed above.

(A recordable offence is any offence held on the Police National Computer. This includes offences punishable by imprisonment and others specified in the National Police Records (Recordable Offences) Regulations 2000.)

You must include spent convictions under the Rehabilitation of Offenders Act 1974 (by virtue of the provisions of the Rehabilitation of Offenders Act 1974 (Exemptions) Order 1975) or any involvement with civil, military or transport police.

Applicants are likely to be rejected if they have been involved in any of the following:

- Offences involving serious violence or injury (including Grievous Bodily Harm (GBH) and Actual Bodily Harm (ABH).

- Offences involving unsolicited violence towards others.

- Unlawful possession of weapons, firearms or going equipped to steal.

- Gross indecency, acts of indecency and abuse or neglect of children.

- Public Order offences – involvement in riot, violent disorder, affray, causing intentional harassment, alarm or distress.

- Racially motivated or homophobic offences

Equality and Diversity
"Equality is not about treating everybody the same, but recognising we are all individuals, unique in our own way. Equality and fairness is about recognising, accepting and valuing people's unique individuality according to their needs.

This often means that individuals may be treated appropriately, yet fairly, based on their needs."

Members of the community need to trust their Police Officers and be confident that they will be respected and treated fairly by them.

This is particularly true of ethnic minority communities. It is of vital importance that a Police Service represents the community in which it serves. This means that a diverse community needs a diverse Police Force in order to give it the best service possible.

Police Officers from ethnic groups are far better positioned to understand the needs of ethnic communities, which is why the Police Service encourages applicants from every background.

The Police Service is an equal opportunities employer and encourages diversity at every level and every role. They are keen to see more ethnic minority officers move through the ranks to higher levels - but all promotion is on merit. They are looking, therefore, for able people with the ambition and drive to move onwards and upwards.

The police have in recent years come under great criticism for their lack of ability to handle cultural issues and for their lack of black and Asian Officers. However, they have been working hard to improve this problem and are very keen to employ people from all cultures and backgrounds.

It is important that the Police Force represents the community that it serves so that it can provide the best possible service to everyone.

The police are keen to encourage more minority ethnic applicants as well as more women, and stress their commitment

to creating a diverse force that best reflect the varied communities it serves. We live in an increasingly diverse community and it is of vital importance that you understand and believe in the need for diversity in the Police Force before you apply.

Under the Race Relations (Amendment) Act, public authorities (Including the

Police Force) have a general duty to promote race equality. This means that when carrying out their functions or duties they must have due regard to the need to:

- Eliminate unlawful discrimination;

- Promote equality of opportunity;

- Promote good relations between persons of different racial groups.

In order to demonstrate how a Police Force plan to meet their statutory duties they have an obligation to produce and publish a Race Equality Scheme. The Race Equality Scheme outlines their strategy and action plan to ensure that equality and diversity are mainstreamed through their policies, practices, procedures and functions.

Central to this strategy are external consultation, monitoring and assessment, training, and ensuring that the public has access to this information. It is advised that you are aware of the Race Equality Scheme for the individual Police Force that you are applying to. By doing this you will have learnt a considerable amount about this important topic before you join the Police Force and also, more importantly, demonstrate a commitment to Equality and Fairness.

EQUALITY AND FAIRNESS - THE SELECTION PROCESS

During the Police selection process you will be assessed in the area of equality and fairness. The core competency that covers this area is as follows:

Respect for Diversity

Considers and shows respect for the opinions, circumstances and feelings of colleagues and members of the public, no matter what their position, background, circumstances, status or appearance.

How to Meet the Core Competency

Demonstrate that you understand other people's views and take them into account. Show that you are tactful and diplomatic when dealing with people, and that you are capable of treating people with dignity and respect at all times, no matter what their background, status, circumstances or appearance.

Positive Indicators

- Sees issues from other people's viewpoints;

- Treats everyone with respect and dignity;

- Is polite, tolerant and patient when dealing with people;

- Respects the needs of everyone involved when sorting out disagreements;

- Shows understanding and sensitivity to people's problems, vulnerabilities and needs;

- Makes people feel valued by listening to and supporting their needs and interests;

- Uses language in an appropriate way and is sensitive to the way it may affect people;

- Identifies and respects other people's values within the law;

- Understands what offends others and takes this into account;

- Respects confidentiality, wherever appropriate;

- Delivers difficult messages honestly and sensitively; Is open and honest with people.

We mention this fact on a number of occasions throughout this guide but you must read, learn, absorb and understand the core competencies relevant to each section. The 'Respecting Diversity' core competency covers the areas indicated on the previous page.

During your responses try to include some of the 'Positive Indicators' that we have listed. For example, when dealing with an incident that involves equality and fairness issues make sure you are sensitive to people's needs. Treat everyone with respect and dignity and see things from others' points of view. Try also to understand what offends people and take this into account when dealing with their problems or needs.

THE ASSESSMENT CENTRE – NATIONAL RECRUITMENT ASSESSMENT CENTRE

Once you have successfully passed the 'Application Form' stage of the process you will be invited to attend an assessment centre. The assessment centre location will vary from force to force but you will be provided with details, times and location. Make sure you know exactly where your venue is and don't be late! The assessment centre will provide information regarding your suitability for recruitment into the Police Service.

The assessment centre is usually conducted over a period of five hours. For the assessment centre you will be required to take a number of important documents with you to confirm your identification to the Police:

A full 10 year passport or TWO of the following:

- British Driving Licence;

- P45;

- Birth Certificate, issued within six weeks of birth;

- Cheque Book and Bank Card with three statements and proof of signature;

- Card containing a photograph of yourself;

- Proof of residence, e.g. Council Tax, Gas, Electricity, Water or Telephone Bill.

Make sure that you read the information given to you and take along the relevant documents as if you do not, then you won't be able to continue with the day.

At the assessment centre you will be required to undertake a numerical reasoning test, a verbal reasoning test, written exercises, interactive/role play exercises and a structured interview. In the numerical reasoning test you may be asked to answer multiple choice questions that will measure your ability to solve numerical problems accurately.

In the verbal logical reasoning test you will be asked to answer multiple choice questions that will measure your ability to reason logically when given facts about events. In the written and interactive exercises, you may have to assume the role of a newly appointed Customer Services Officer at a fictitious retail and leisure complex.

During the interview you may be asked questions about how you have dealt with situations in your past and we have provided you with in depth information to help you pass this stage in a separate section of this guide. You will be given an information pack, which you must read and familiarise yourself with all of its content.

THE APPLICATION FORM

How you complete the application form is very important as you must pass this stage before progressing through to the following stages. You should spend plenty of time in preparing your answers to 'specific' questions on the application form. You will be asked to complete a number of sections, which include your personal details such as address, previous addresses, date of birth and qualifications to name just a few.

This is the simple part of the application form but you can still fail these sections if you don't follow the instructions given.

TIP 1: Check to see what colour ink they ask you to complete the form in because if you get this part wrong you may possibly fail. If it asks for black ink then make certain you complete in black and not blue.

TIP 2: Practice first! It is a good idea to complete the application as a rough copy first just in case you make mistakes. Also make sure you photocopy your completed application form because you will need this to make reference to if you progress through the selection process.

Some application forms will have a section asking you *'Why do you want to join this particular force?'*

This is an important part of the application form and it is your chance to 'sell yourself'. Try to think of the reasons why you want to join and be honest. Remember that the Police Force is not just there to bring criminals to justice and whilst it may appear to be exciting catching criminals the Police Force is to there to serve the community. Also remember that most Police Forces operate a 'Community based approach', which means that they respond to the needs of the community in which they serve.

We also advise that you visit the website of the Police Force you are applying to join and learn as much about their work as possible. When completing this part of the form try to think about what the role of a Police Officer is when constructing your answer.

You will be asked a number of questions on the application form and on the following pages we have provided you with some tips and advice on how to approach these questions. Please remember that these are provided as a guide only and you should base your answers around your own experiences in both work life and personal life.

Sample Question from the Police Application Form:
Q. WHAT KNOWLEDGE, SKILLS AND EXPERIENCES DO YOU HAVE THAT WILL ENABLE YOU TO MEET THE REQUIREMENTS OF A POLICE OFFICER?

Questions based around 'Knowledge, skills and experience' are looking for you to demonstrate that you can meet the requirements of the 'person specification' for the job you are applying for. Therefore, your answer should match these as closely as possible. Your first step is to find out what the 'person specification' is for the particular force you are applying to join. Essentially, the role of a Police Officer is made up of seven 'core competencies'.

Basically you are looking to match your responses with the Police Officer core competencies. Once you have found the 'core competencies', now is the time to structure your answer around these, ensuring that you briefly cover each area based upon your own experiences in both your work life and personal life.

THE PERSON SPECIFICATION – CORE COMPETENCIES

The core competencies that form the basis of the Police Officer role are as follows:

• **Respect for race and diversity**

Considers and shows respect for the opinions, circumstances and feelings of colleagues and members of the public no matter what their race, religion, position, background, circumstances, status or appearance.

• **Team working**

Develops strong working relationships inside and outside the team to achieve common goals. Breaks down barriers between groups and involves others in discussions and decisions.

• **Community and Customer Focus**

Focuses on the customer and provides a high-quality service that is tailored to meet their individual needs. Understands the community that is served and shows an active commitment to policing that reflects the needs and concerns of the community.

• **Effective Communication**

Communicates ideas and information effectively, both verbally and in writing. Uses language and a style of

communication that is appropriate to the situation and people being addressed. Makes sure that others understand what is going on.

- **Problem Solving**

  Gathers information from a range of sources. Analyses information to identify problems and issues, and makes effective decisions.

- **Personal Responsibility**

  Takes personal responsibility for making things happen and achieving results. Displays motivation, commitment, perseverance and conscientiousness. Acts with a high degree of integrity.

- **Resilience**

  Shows resilience, even in difficult circumstances. Prepared to make difficult decisions and has the confidence to see them through.

THE ASSESSMENT CENTRE

Interactive Exercises

During the 4 interactive exercises you may need to deal with specific situations along the following lines:

- A manager of a store that is inside the leisure complex wants to discuss a security issue with you;

- A customer wants to talk to you about an interaction with another customer;

- A school teacher would like to discuss an issue with you regarding his/her pupils;

- A centre worker would like to discuss an issue with you.

Once again remember the core competencies that you have studied in your pack when you are making your responses.

- Have respect for people's views and feelings;

- See issues from others' point of view;

- Listen to their needs and interests;

- Respect confidentiality where appropriate;

- Present an appropriate image to the public;

- Try to sort out customers problems as soon as possible.

TOP TIPS

A good way to practice for these exercises is to get a friend or family relative to 'role play' a similar situation to one of the above. Try to pick someone you know who will make it difficult for you and try to resolve their issue in a calm but effective manner in line with the core competencies that you will have been given.

There will normally be four interactive exercises that you will be assessed against. This part of the selection process will be split into two five minute parts. The first part will consist of the preparation phase and the second part will be the actual activity phase that you'll be assessed against.

The Preparation Phase

During the 5 minute preparation phase you will be provided with the actual scenario either on a card or sheet of paper. You will be taken to a desk or separate room where you will have 5 minutes to prepare for the actual test. You will be allowed to take notes during the preparation and then use them during the activity phase. Please note that the preparation phase is not assessable. Once your 5 minutes is complete you will then be taken to the activity area and the assessment will begin.

Make sure you take your preparation notes and information with you. Before we move onto the activity stage let's take a look at how you can use the preparation time wisely. On the following page we have provided you with a sample exercise.

IMPORTANT – YOU WILL BE ASSESSED AGAINST RESPECT AND DIVERSITY DURING EVERY EXERCISE OR SCENARIO.

SAMPLE INTERACTIVE EXERCISES

EXERCISE 1

You are the Customer Service Manager at a fictitious retail centre. A member of your staff approaches you and tells you that she has been sexually harassed by another member of staff. The woman is clearly upset by the situation and wants you to take action.

How to Prepare

To begin with you should study the 'MAIN DUTIES AND RESPONSIBILITIES' of your role. What do they say about the level of customer service, resolving complaints, meeting the equality policy and ensuring high standards etc. Do any of them relate to the scenario? If so take note of them and make sure you meet them during the activity stage. Now look at the Equality Policy.

Is any of the information contained in the policy relevant to the scenario? If so then take note of it and make sure you meet the standards of the policy during the activity stage. Finally, take a look at the Code of Conduct section. Again, does any of it apply to the scenario? If so take notes and ensure you meet the requirements during the activity stage.

TOP TIP

Read the information pack prior to attending the assessment centre and know it inside out!!

THE ACTIVITY PHASE – EXERCISE 1

During the activity stage you will be assessed on what you did and how you did it. You will be graded from A to D with the highest score earning you an A to the weakest score earning you a D. Obviously you want to aim for an A but don't be disheartened if you feel that you haven't done well on a particular exercise as you can make up for it in another.

Exercise 1 focuses on a complaint made by a member of staff who claims that she has been sexually harassed by another member of staff. Within the equality policy statement you will find suggested courses of action. The options here may suggest that the person asks the offender to stop, the problem is discussed with an appropriate person (you) or the option is available to make a formal complaint. On the following page we have provided you with some suggested responses. Most of these can be applied to similar exercises surrounding harassment cases although you should judge every situation separately and act according to the brief.

Additional Guidance
- Remember never to get annoyed or show signs of anger during the interactive exercises;

- The members of staff who are carrying out the fictitious roles will try to make the situation difficult to deal with. They may come across in a confrontational manner during the scenario role plays so be prepared for this. Don't let it put you on the back foot and remember that they are trying to test your ability to defuse confrontational situations;

- Most importantly, make sure you remember to respect equality and diversity at all times. You will be assessed in this area during every scenario;

- Finally, remember to be confident and firm whenever required. However, do respect your role as a customer service manager and provide a high level of service.

SAMPLE ENGLISH TEST - QUESTION 1

A fire has occurred in a nightclub belonging to Harry James. One person died in the fire, which occurred at 11pm on Saturday night. The club was insured for less than its value.

QUESTIONS – TRUE, FALSE OR IMPOSSIBLE TO SAY

1. The fire occurred at 1100 hours.

2. A relative of Harry James was killed in the fire.

3. If the insurance company decide to pay out for the fire, Harry James stands to make a profit.

4. The fire was caused by arson.

5. The club was not insured at the time of the fire.

SAMPLE NUMERACY TESTS - EXERCISE 1

1. A wallet has been found containing one £20 note, five £5 notes, a fifty pence coin and three 2 pence coins. How much is in the wallet?

2. Subtract 200 from 500, add 80, subtract 30 and multiply by 2. What number do you have?

3. A multi-storey car park has 8 floors and can hold 72 cars on each floor. In addition to this there is also allocation for 4 disabled parking spaces per floor. How many spaces are there in the entire car park?

4. A man saves £12.50 per month. How much would he have saved after 1 year?

5. If there have been 60 accidents along one stretch of a

motorway in the last year, how many, on average, have occurred each month?

ANSWERS TO ENGLISH TEST - QUESTION 1
1. FALSE

2. IMPOSSIBLE TO SAY

3. FALSE

4. IMPOSSIBLE TO SAY

5. FALSE

ANSWERS TO NUMERACY QUESTIONS – EXERCISE 1
QUESTION 1: £45.56

QUESTION 2: 700

QUESTION 3: 608

QUESTION 4: £150

QUESTION 5: 5

THE WRITTEN EXERCISES

During the assessment centre you will be asked to undertake 2 written exercises. The written exercise will either be in the form of a report, letter, memo or proposal. During the written exercise it is essential that you limit your spelling mistakes as you are only allowed to make 10 in total so avoid choosing words that you find difficult to spell. When you are preparing your responses it is important to remember the 'core competencies', which you will have studied when you received your information pack. Try to structure your answers in a professional manner and listen to what is required. On the following pages we have provided you with a sample written exercise question for you to try. You should assume the role of Customer Services Officer at the Westshire Centre. Read the memorandum and the extract from the appraisal and use a blank sheet of to formulate your report.

WRITING A LETTER

Writing a letter, especially if it is in response to a complaint, can be quite a difficult task. However, with a little bit of preparation and practice you can improve your communication skills greatly. Try to imagine that you are the manager of a leisure centre or other similar complex. You receive a letter of complaint from a disgruntled member of the public. How do you respond?

Obviously you need to be professional and impartial in your response, taking into account the customer's needs following their bad experience. Why do you need to do this? The answer is simple – you are providing a service to that particular customer and they feel you have let them down. Of course it is important to investigate the complaint to ensure its validity but in relation to dealing with complaints you must

try to resolve the issue carefully and effectively. Take a look at the letter of complaint on the following page.

PREPARING A WRITTEN RESPONSE

After speaking to the receptionist she admits to becoming impatient with the lady because her English was very poor and it was a very busy day with lots of customers to serve. She says that the telephones kept ringing too and she'd not had a break for over 3 hours. So you've gathered your information and confirmed that the complaint is a genuine one. How do you deal with it? You have a number of choices when compiling your response. Do you think it is wise to explain it was a busy period for the receptionist at that time and she had not had a break for a while?

The answer should be NO. The problems at the leisure centre in relation to the complaint are purely down to a management issue. There should be enough staff on the reception to deal with the majority of eventualities including telephone calls, bookings and taking payments so it is not wise to make any excuses in your letter to the complainant. When compiling your response you need to think of the core competencies and compose your letter in relation to them. In respect of this particular scenario there is no excuse for the receptionist's behaviour and obviously there is a training issue that needs to be resolved. Your letter, therefore, should reflect the fact that you accept responsibility for the poor customer service the complainant has experienced. On the following page we have compiled a sample response.

After reading the sample response letter do you think it is an appropriate response? The way to ascertain if your responses are correct is to match them against the core competencies relevant to that of a Police Officer. On the following page we

have tried to demonstrate how we believe we have achieved this. Whatever letter or response you have to compile during the assessment centre you should always try to match the core competencies, which ultimately means you will have to spend time learning them prior to your assessment centre day. Everybody has different ways of learning but some of the most effective ways may include:

- Writing the core competencies down every day for 3 weeks prior to your assessment day.

- Reading them at least once every day 3 weeks prior to your assessment day.

- Carrying a small card around with you that has all of the core competencies written out on them. Whenever you get a spare few minutes get the card out and read them.

- Get someone to test you twice a week on the core competencies.

MATCHING THE CORE COMPETENCIES

Matching the Police Officer core competencies can be a difficult task unless you know them in depth, which is why you need to spend time learning them. Of course you don't want to be so engrossed in them that you forget to be yourself on the day but nonetheless they should form the basis of your preparation. It is also a good idea to practice writing letters correctly in terms of your grammar, punctuation and spelling.

Remember that one of the Police core competencies is to COMMUNICATE EFFECTIVELY both in terms of verbal and written form, so a little practice in this area will go a long way. Another good way to practice your written responses is to formulate your own letter of complaint or get a family

relative, friend or partner to write a fictitious one for you to respond to. The more you practice the better you will become at matching the core competencies. Please remember that the written response you may have to reply to during the assessment centre will not necessarily be a complaint. Whatever you are responding to just remember to try and match the core competencies.

TIPS FOR PASSING THE WRITTEN EXERCISES

Pay attention to the brief provided from the recruitment staff. Listen to what they are saying and follow their instructions. You only have 20 minutes per exercise in which to read all of the information and to create a written response. Work fast but remember to be accurate. Keep the number of spelling mistakes and grammar errors to an absolute minimum. You will lose marks for errors. In order to achieve higher marks use the documentation to provide suggestions as to how the issue could be addressed and also explain the reason for your suggestions. Deal with the issue in a considerate and constructive manner. Do not be inconsiderate or dismissive in your response. Try to use keywords in your response that match the core competencies.

THE INTERVIEW

The final stage of the Police selection process is the interview. Under normal circumstances the board will consist of up to 3 senior police officers. It is important to remember that whilst you will be nervous don't let this get in the way of your success. Police Officers, in general are confident people who have the ability to rise to a challenge and perform under difficult and pressurised situations. Treat the interview no differently to this.

You are capable of becoming a Police Officer and the nerves that you have on the day are only natural, in fact they will help you to perform better if you have prepared sufficiently. The Police interview board will have a number of set questions to choose from and whilst these are constantly changing they will form part of the Police Officer core competencies. Before attending your interview ensure that you read, digest and understand the Police core competencies. Without these it will be difficult to pass the interview.

On the following pages we have provided you with a number of possible interview questions and answers to help you understand the types of questions you will be up against. Remember that these are examples only and you should not treat these as the definitive questions that you will be asked on the day of your interview.

The interview will last for approximately 30-60 minutes in which you will be asked a number of questions about specific situations and experiences that are important to the role of the Police Officer.

These questions will be based around the core competencies. Here are four examples that have been used in the past:

RESPECT FOR DIVERSITY;

TEAMWORKING;

PERSONAL RESPONSIBILITY;

RESILIENCE;

EFFECTIVE COMMUNICATION.

You will be allowed up to 5 minutes to answer each question so don't be afraid to use the time you have. You may find during the interview that the interviewer asks you probing questions. These are designed to help you in giving your response so listen to what he or she has to say.

PREPARING FOR THE INTERVIEW

You may find it useful to think of examples you may be able to use in the interview prior to attending the assessment centre. In your 'welcome pack', which will be sent to you approximately 2 weeks before the date of your assessment centre, you should find examples of the 'core competencies relevant to a police constable'. These are the criteria that you will be scored against so it is worthwhile reading them beforehand and trying to structure your answers around them as best you can.

For example, one of the sections you will be assessed against is 'Respect for Diversity'. You may be asked a question where you have to give an example of where you have had to respect other people's opinions and views which are from a different culture or background than yourself.

Try to think of an example where you have had to do this and structure your answer around the core competencies required, e.g. you are respectful to people and treat them with dignity whilst taking into consideration their views and opinions. You are sensitive to language and use it in an appropriate manner etc. Within the core competencies are the 'negative indicators'. Make sure when answering your questions you avoid these as much as possible.

Another of the areas that you will be assessed against is 'Personal Responsibility'. Again, take time to read the core competencies given and try to understand what the assessment panel are looking for. They are looking for examples of where you have taken personal responsibility for making something happen, something where you have displayed motivation, commitment, perseverance and integrity. Take the time to think of a good strong example where you have demonstrated all of the competencies required. On the

following page we have provided you with an example of how your response can be structured. We have then indicated the words that we believe are 'hitting' the core competencies required.

THE POLICE INTERVIEW – TIPS AND ADVICE

- The Police may ask you more generic questions relating to your past experiences or skills. These may be in relation to solving problems, working as an effective team member, dealing with difficult or aggressive people and defusing confrontational situations. Make sure you have examples for each of these.

- Try to speak to a current serving Police Officer of the force that you are applying to join. Ask him/her what it is like to work for that particular force and what the current policing issues are. From their feedback take the positive points but don't use any detrimental or negative feedback during the interview.

- Try to think of a time when you have made a mistake and how you learnt from the experience.

- When you complete the application form make sure you keep a copy of it. Before you go to your interview ensure that you read the application form over and over again as you may find you are asked questions about your responses.

- Don't be afraid to ask the interviewer to repeat a question if you do not hear it the first time. Take your time when answering and be measured in your responses.

- If you don't know the answer to a question then be honest and just say 'I don't know'. This is far better than trying

to answer a question that you have no knowledge about. Conversely, if your answer to a question is challenged there is nothing wrong with sticking to your point but make sure you acknowledge the interviewer's thoughts or views. Be polite and never get into a debate.

• You will be scored against the current Police core competencies so make sure you try to structure your answers accordingly. The Police core competencies are the first thing you should learn during your preparation.

THE POLICE INTERVIEW - FAQS

How long will my interview last?

Of course this very much depends on how long your responses are.

Generally the interview will last between 30 – 60 minutes.

Do you think I should ask questions at the end of my interview?

This can't do any harm providing that the questions aren't inappropriate or harmful to your chances of success. Questions such as "Thank you for taking the time to interview me, can you tell me what the next stage is please?" are satisfactory questions. However, questions such as "I have read that the Police Force in this area have been criticised for their poor crime reduction figures lately, what are they going to do about it?" are definitely not advised. Do not try to be clever!

I've heard that there are sometimes up to 5 people on the interview panel. Is this true?

No, we have never heard of any instances where 5 people are on the interview panel. There are usually only 2 or 3 at the most.

Is it ok to use 'body language' during my interview to express myself?

Yes, most definitely. Using your hands or facial expression during any interview is a positive aspect as it demonstrates confidence. However, there is a fine line between subtle expression and overdoing it. If it becomes too obvious then it can be off putting for the panel. Try sitting in front of a mirror and practice saying the reasons why you want to become a Police Officer. This will give you an idea of what the panel will be looking at during your interview.

What are the criteria for passing the Police interview?

Don't get tied down or concerned with specific pass marks or pass rates.

The Police will score you primarily against the core competencies. Try to structure your responses to the interview questions around the core competencies and you will score points every time you do.

You may find some of the following phrases useful when constructing your answers:

- Dignity and respect;
- Team working;
- Strong working relationships;
- Effective team member;
- Achieving common goals;
- Customer focus;

- Community policing;

- Sensitive to cultural issues;

- Sensitive towards racial differences;

- Presenting the right image to the public;

- Effective communication;

- Identify problems and make effective decisions;

- Motivated, conscientious and committed;

- Calm, considerate and can work well under pressure.

TOP TIPS

Be smart. Tidy hair, clean shoes, suit etc all create a good image.

Also spend time sitting upright in a chair at home and pretend that you are being interviewed. Even ask a member of your family to interview you with the questions contained in this guide to help you get a feel of being under pressure.

When answering your questions respond to the panel as opposed to the person who has asked you the question. Make eye contact with the members of the panel as opposed to looking at the floor. However, don't be aggressive in your eye contact.

ADDITIONAL ADVICE

Sit in the chair upright at all times and do not slouch. Smile, whenever possible and be confident. Rest the palms of your hands on your knees when you are not using them to express yourself and keep your feet flat on the ground.

CHAPTER 7
BECOME A POLICE DOG HANDLER

YOUR DREAM JOB

Some people dream to not only be a Police Officer, but to be in charge of what they believe is the ultimate criminal-catching arm of the Law – the Police Dog. In order to make their dream come true they must join the police, go through the basic training and acquire the necessary skills to become a police officer. This will involve two years on patrol as a Police Constable.

Two years later, on their sergeant's recommendation, they can apply to train to be a dog handler. The **competition is tough,** as there are **only a few dog handlers** in each police force. There is a test, carrying out tasks with the dogs. This could involve acting as the 'criminal' and allowing the dog to hold and detain – with its teeth! There is no room for being timid around dogs if this is the dream.

If successful, there may be the offer of a place, but there are no promises. A lot depends on the abilities of the applicant and their desire, as well as the available places to work with the dogs.

It is a very worthwhile job, both in the rewards of keeping the peace and in doing a good work, and in having a close relationship with a canine friend and co-worker.

The training course involves practical work, but also classroom work and lectures. There is a lot to be learned in order to become a police dog handler. Officers deemed suitable for training are carefully selected, as their work with the dogs is vital to the police. A dog and its handler will work together as a team. They are matched for the purpose, and the handler choice is just as important as the selection of his or her dog.

Potential police dog *officers must be experienced as policemen or women*, with an even temper and mental alertness, and the willingness to go beyond the expected.

It is vital that you have demonstrated these qualities in your previous years as a serving officer as this will be taken into account when considering you for this position. Although you maybe told that every applicant is equal your previous actions will be taken into account!

A police dog handler will be responsible not only for their own safety on the job, but also for the safety and handling of their colleague dog. This is as the colleague dog will rely on the handler totally for all its needs. A police dog handler will also need to be *physically capable of the high demands of the job*, with strength and stamina almost equal to the dog.

There may be some advantage in having had experience in handling animals and particularly dogs, but a suitable officer who has the desire to learn to work with dogs could well be

eligible to train as a police dog handler. The most important qualification would seem to be a *cheerful attitude and an easygoing manner*, which will bring a positive response from a dog and will actually encourage the good behaviour of a dog. Anyone with an abrupt manner who is not flexible or doesn't show the desire to work will not mix well with dog handling.

As police dogs are kennelled at the handlers' homes, anyone who wishes to become a handler *must have a secure and amenable environment for the dog.*

KEY POINT: If you want to become a police dog handler you cannot live in a flat.

Your home will be inspected to ensure that you can provide a suitable living location for your dog. Ideally you will need adequate space outside to keep and maintain a kennel and dog.

A potential dog handler must prove his or her devotion to the dog and their commitment to their duties. The dog's attitude to work will be a reflection of its handler's attitude, and they will share a confidence and respect for each other. Obviously, a potential handler's ability with a dog can only be seen once he or she has been paired with a dog and they have become familiar with each other or commenced training together.

WHY DOGS?

Police have found that they can rely on dogs, particularly their powers of smell and hearing. Humans cannot do the work of dogs when it comes to sniffing out drugs, weapons, cash or criminals. Dogs are also very good at chasing and catching suspects or at finding lost things or people. However, they can also be a colleague who will protect their handler and give their lives if required.

Police dog handler training involves complete dedication and commitment for both the officer and the dog, and their working relationship can last for 7 years of working and living together. Some handlers keep their working dog past the dog's retirement age, because they are such good companions. The handler is responsible for the health and wellbeing of the dog throughout its working life and usually after the dog has retired.

Those police dog handlers who have made this commitment are enjoying a fulfilling and exciting career. They are challenged every day with new experiences. It's not a run-of-the-mill job, with great physical effort being required, and mostly outdoor work. Hours of work vary according to the jobs to be carried out, and the pay for the commitment and hard work can be up to £25,000 per year.

DUTIES OF THE HANDLER

The handler is always responsible for the control of his dog, whether on or off the lead. As a result, when the dog is off the lead care must be taken that the dog remains in sight, or at least hearing distance, as much as possible. The handler must always be able to recall the dog if necessary.

Control of the Police Dog

It is a handler's responsibility to maintain control of his or her dog at all times, on duty and off. The dog is capable of independent thought and action, even when well trained, so total control is not achievable. However, through the training process, the handler learns to impose his will on the dog, so that the dog's first thought becomes obedience rather than disobedience. It is important for the handler to be able to maintain control over the dog especially in stressful situations, of which there are many. The two main types of control are outlined below:

1. On the Lead

The lead is used at the beginning of training, in order to assist the dog in learning how to carry out the commands. The length of the lead can be controlled by the handler, so that the distance between the dog and the handler can be extended or shortened, depending on need. As the dog learns the various commands, the handler can also use the lead to control the moving direction of the dog, for example, side-to-side movement in front of a crowd, or back and forth when training the dog to 'fetch' and 'retrieve'. However, the handler may not be able to control any spontaneous actions of crowds or individuals, or a spontaneous reaction from the dog in certain situations. These are responses that can be instilled into a well-trained dog.

2. Off the Lead

Once the handler knows that the dog has learned to carry out a command, he can take the dog off the lead and allow it to do its work without physical restrictions. This will be necessary when the dog is to search inside a building or vehicle or in an open area. The handler must trust the dog to continue carrying out his command, despite the fact that the dog might come up against things beyond the handler's control. He needs to know that his dog will respond in the correct manner

THE ROLE

The police dog handler works with his or her canine colleague to:

- Assist the police in the detection of crime;

- Locate offenders;

- Search for drugs, stolen goods, cash, weapons, explosives or lost items;

- Search for lost people or bodies;

- Control crowds;

- Protect colleagues;

- Chase and detain suspects on the run;

- Detection of drugs and illegal substances at airports and train stations.

Skills and Qualities

A police dog handler should be an experienced police officer and should know the legal requirements of his or her job in each situation. He or she should also be prepared to care for and exercise their dog both at home and on duty, always considering its welfare and wellbeing.

A handler needs to develop a good relationship with their dog, know its moods and temperament and know how to deal with them. He or she needs to care for their dog's every need and ensure that the dog knows it can rely on them to care for them and keep them safe and secure.

The team of the handler and the dog needs to work, both with other teams and also independently, without supervision. Communication with other officers and with other dog teams is a must, as is teamwork. Consistence and reliability are all important, as colleagues must depend on one another. A handler must be confident in his or her own abilities, and also in their dog's skills, in order to work well as a team. Due to the fact that most of the working day involves rigorous exercise; the handler must be physically fit and active, and strong enough to control their dog.

A handler should also really want to work with dogs and be

interested in understanding their needs and capabilities. He or she needs to be patient, as working with and looking after a police dog takes a lot of time and effort.

Working together

The type of police dog a handler will work with depends on the types of dogs used by a particular police force and which ones are available for the position. Some police forces have dogs only for certain areas of work, so a handler must be prepared to be flexible and work with their dog in the area of work where it is required.

Police dogs live with their handlers and the officer must feed, groom and exercise his or her dog. Some handlers also decide to keep the dog as their own once the dog is retired from working life, so this is something a potential handler may wish to consider for the future.

Working conditions

Hours may be long and unsociable, including nights and weekends, and handlers are required to be flexible in what is needed. Although the work may involve a lot of waiting around and standing for long periods, there is also active duty which includes walking for miles and also running very fast! Most of the work is outdoors and in all types of weather, so again flexibility and adaptability are a necessity for the job.

Salaries are usually on a set scale for the police force, but a police dog handler can earn up to £25,000 per year.

A DAY IN THE LIFE OF A POLICE DOG HANDLER

A typical day for a Police Dog Handler might include the following:

Role

The handler and his or her dog work together to assist and support police officers, perhaps in searching for suspects (as in the case of when the dog is a German Shepherd as they are very good at searching for people). A trained police dog has a sense of smell and hearing that can detect things humans or cameras can't, like property that has been thrown down, and left or missing persons. The handler and dog attend public events, like sporting events, to be a visual warning for expected troublemakers or antisocial behaviour. They also are available to respond to situations that may arise, such as firearm or domestic violence incidents.

Main Responsibilities

The handler's main responsibility is his or her dog's welfare and training, both at work and at home. There is exercising the dog, grooming it, cleaning out the kennel, transporting it to and from work and ensure the dog is ready for duty. Each dog is trained for a different role and they can detect different things, such as firearms, drugs and explosives. German Shepherds are general purpose dogs, so they can be used to help in search and rescue missions or to control large crowds, as well as helping to chase and detain suspects fleeing from the scene of a crime.

If a team of dog and handler are not actively training or responding to incidents, they proactively patrol areas, which could mean being on the beat in high crime areas, being on the lookout for known criminals or watching for drug dealers, and so on. They also give education and crime-prevention support within local communities.

If someone goes missing, the Dog Unit are called in to help. German Shepherd dogs are mostly used for tracking as they are so skilled at following a human scent even over a large

area. By following the scent and the handler's commands, a German Shepherd can very quickly find a person and alert its handler to the position.

Dogs can also find property that has been stolen but dropped or hidden in the thief's hurry to escape. They are also able to find cash, usually because the thieves leave a human scent on anything that they have handled. When suspects try and outrun the police officer, the dog can easily apprehend them. Often just seeing a menacing police dog can stop the most disorderly of crowds and so as a result dogs are often used to calm disruptions.

Hours of Duty

Most dog units operate a certain number of weeks on a rolling shift pattern, so to provide police cover when it's required. Therefore there are early shifts, late shifts and night shifts, all 7 days of the week.

Working Environment

City areas are mostly restricted to certain districts, rather than the whole city. However, a team of dog and handler may be required to respond to an incident within the whole county area, depending on the need of police presence and the specific need for dog teams. There are quiet moments and dog handlers can use these times for role play with their dogs, so always keeping on top of every possibility.

Working Teams

Dog teams are part of the police response and investigation teams. There are firearm and air support units, as well as drug teams, search and rescue teams and crowd control teams.

Skills and Qualities of the Handler

A dog handler must be prepared to exercise and care for the dog on duty and off duty. He or she must be an experienced police officer, so as to know the operational and legal implications involved at each incident. A handler must obviously be confident around dogs. Because of the physical exertion required, including sometimes lifting a dog over fences, a handler must be physically fit.

Why this Work?

A person may have had experience of police work through a school's work experience programme, or discovered a website describing the job of police dog handler, or perhaps have known a friend or relative who is a police dog handler. There is obviously a keenness to want to work with dogs and an affinity with the police and the work that they do for someone to consider this type of work.

Training

Someone who is hoping to become a police dog handler must be a police officer in the first instance. The minimum time to be a constable is for the two-year probation period. The more years spent as a constable gives further experience in situations and therefore will be a better background and give more opportunity to actually achieve the role of police dog handler. There is a rigorous application and interview process, as well as a house check, and then the two-week suitability course, which some people find to be the hardest part of the training.

This is where a potential handler learns how to train the dog and everything he or she needs to know about dogs and their care and even the psychology of dogs. Once through this initial training, the handler then attends a 12-week course at a dog training school with his or her dog, bonding

and nurturing the relationship between them, making them an inseparable team. Even an experienced handler will have to go through the 12-week course again every time he or she has a new dog. Training on the job is continuous through-out the dog's working life, ensuring that 16 training days are completed every year.

Tools for the Job

Each activity may require a different dog collar or lead. There is a special tracking harness with a 9-metre line which gives the dog the freedom to track and search, still under the han-dler's control. During bite training, protective sleeves must be worn.

Job Joys

Police dog handlers talk about the rush of adrenaline when they know they are nearing the capture of a suspect. The dog's hard work makes this possible, and the dog enjoys this part of the job probably even more than the handler. It's the dog's instinct that enables it to scent, track, hunt and capture the fleeing suspect.

Challenges

It's important to be in the right place at the right time. With-out the skills of the dog and the good training of the handler, it would be easy to miss out on getting to an incident while the offender is still in the area. The physicality of the work is also a challenge, as the handler and the dog must always keep up the training and the exercise in order to be on top of the job.

Future

Most police dog handlers love their work and want to keep doing it as long as they can. Attachments between handlers and dogs are natural and are able to continue when the dog

retires, as long as the handler can bring it home to stay. The handler will then go on to train and work with another dog, starting the process all over again.

Advice
One police dog handler gave some tips for those who are considering this role:

- Work hard and get a few years of experience as a police constable before considering training as a police dog handler. You will then gain the insight and skills you will need.

- You could also train to be a dog handler through the Armed Forces and other organisations, but to work day-by-day as a handler, a career with the police is the best way to go.

Application for position
Applicants for the role of police dog handler must have lived in the UK for 3 years immediately prior to submission of an application. Anyone who is not a UK or EC citizen must also have indefinite leave to remain in the UK. If a member of the UK Armed Forces or of the Foreign or Commonwealth office diplomatic community applies for a position of police dog handler, they must have lived in the UK for at least 3 years at some point, even if they are not presently resident in the UK. Applicants who have never lived in the UK are not eligible.

Candidates who do not match the 'essential' criteria of the job requirements are unlikely to be invited for interview. If a candidate has a record of poor attendance in their present job, they would probably not progress any further in the selection process. Periods of absence from work due to sickness of more than 12 working days or 4 periods of absence in 12 months would need explanation for consideration by the short-listing panel. Most Constabularies are positive about disabled applicants, although a candidate

must clearly demonstrate that he or she is able to meet the essential criteria for the post.

How to Start

The police force only accepts candidates for dog handling who are already police officers. There is **high competition for this position, so a lot depends on the candidate's accomplishments as an officer and his or her willingness to go through further rigorous training**. Some forces have more availability for dog handlers than others, as the number of police dogs is limited to the requirements of each force. It also is a question of one of the places being available to be filled by a candidate.

The minimum requirement is for a candidate to have completed his or her two-year probationary period. However, the longer an officer has served, the more experience he or she will have had and the more opportunities to have proved skills and abilities in different situations.

SUMMARY OF THE POLICE DOG HANDLER RECRUITMENT PROCESS

To begin from the very beginning, someone wanting to become a police dog handler will need:

- GCSEs

- A-levels (this helps, but is not a requirement to actually become a police officer)

- Police constable of 2 years' standing (out of probation)

- 2-3 years of further experience as a police constable (again this helps but is not a requirement)

- Application to become a police dog handler Interview

- House check for required kennelling for a dog
- Possible 2-week suitability course (not applicable to every police force)
- Police Dog Handler training course of 12 weeks
- Police Dog Handler – finally!
- On going training and refreshers courses

It's not an easy or short journey to become a police dog handler, but those who have gone down the road have found a job that they enjoy and would do it again in order to have the satisfaction and experience they now have. Those that go onto to become a dog handler tend to stick with this career until they retire!

THE METROPOLITAN POLICE FORCE – DOG HANDLER RECRUITMENT PROCESS

A police officer must have completed their two year probationary period as a uniformed officer and have a settled home environment in which to bring the dog into. The candidate will then need to submit an application and be approved by the board of senior officers. They will then undertake an interview and following this attend a one week suitability course to ensure that they possess the correct temperament to work with dogs. If the candidate is not deemed suitable then they will not progress to the next stage.

If they successfully complete the one week suitability course they are allocated a puppy which is usually 8 weeks old. The puppy then lives with the dog handler and becomes part of the family in order to develop a relationship of trust. There are the monthly visits to Keston to check on the puppy's development until the puppy is 10 months old. Handlers are

also taught about problems and issues that can arise and how to deal with them.

At the age of 10 months both the handler and the puppy attend a 5 day course to test the handler's ability. Once the dog has reached 12 months they will begin the initial dog training course where the dog is trained for 12 weeks. The aim is for the dog to obtain what is known as operational status and at the end of the course both the handler and the dog are tested to ensure they meet the required standard. If successful the dog and the handler become fully operational.

During their careers as police dog's they receive on going training and evaluation every 4 months and the handler is assessed to ensure the required level is maintained.

Dog Handler Training

This will be covered in another chapter in more detail, but basically the training involves several weeks (usually 12) of intense training for both the handler and the dog. There is also classroom work and lectures as this learning is vital for the handler's well-rounded instruction. This is the 'nitty-gritty' of looking after the dog and its needs and health, the textbook training of commands and the law and everything that will also have a practical workout in the field.

The application form is usually a typical police force application form. If called for an interview, the candidate will be examined by a board of senior police officers to see if he or she can meet the requirements. The decision is not final until a house check has usually been done, and then a suitability course, in which the candidate's actual capability to handle a dog is tested. This also gives further opportunity for the potential handler to find out further if this is the job they want.

Once a handler begins the 12-week training course with the dog matched to him or her, they and the dog will learn together. The newly trained handler will also receive tutoring from an experienced handler before being allowed to go on patrol. He or she would then be required to complete a one-year probationary period. In order to continue to work, a police dog needs to remain licensed and a handler is required to continue with training days every year, together with the dog.

The Selection of Dog Handlers for Training

There has to be a very careful process in selecting police officers who may be suitable for training as dog handlers. This is just as important as the selection of the dogs, perhaps more so. The chosen handler works with the matched dog throughout the training and all through the dog's working life, usually without supervision. It is vital that the handler and the dog are a good team and that their training is assessed completely before they are employed on the job.

For an officer to be considered for training as a dog handler, he or she must be experienced in police work, with a good record of service. They must be mentally alert, of a level temperament and willing to persevere against all odds. Their training and work as a handler and dog team requires high standards and physical fitness above the average abilities.

If someone wants to become a dog handler, he or she does not need to have had previous experience of handling animals, although it would be an advantage. A suitable officer of experience whose desire is to work as a team with a dog would be eligible. The important thing is that the person is flexible and cheerful, patient and determined, for that is the disposition which will determine the behaviour and temperament of their dog to a great extent. Dogs cannot be used

for police work if their handlers are nagging or sharp with them, as they will become confused and their behaviour will become erratic.

Because police dogs are kennelled at their handler's home, there must be a check of the home and surrounding area to ensure that the dog will be secure and comfortable in a high standard of care, with plenty of room for exercise.

The handler and dog become a devoted team throughout their training and the dog's working life. The officer must not only perform his duties as a police officer to the highest standard, but he must relay this attitude to his dog and its work. Without this attention and respect for their work, the team will be more of a liability to the force than an investment.

During the Familiarisation Course before actual training of the handler and dog is commenced, it can be seen whether a particular officer will have the ability to become a police dog handler. It may sometimes be after training has begun that the handler does not make the grade, but it's better to realise that early on rather than when the pair are actually at work, when the training of both is tested to the full.

Tough Selection Process

A police officer applying to be a police dog handler must successfully complete an interview and assessment week and will then attend a basic course. The length of this course depends on the type of dog, as some work done by the police dogs requires longer training than others. Once the basic course has been successfully completed, the officer will then being work, but will attend for continuing assessment and training once a month.

Dog handlers must be officer's with several years (usually at least 2 years) of experience and who then go through a

rigorous selection process before they can become part of the dog team.

The dogs as well as the handlers need to attain high standards, and they dogs must undergo and pass an annual assessment based on a national police dog standard to ensure they are safe and can effectively and confidently carry out the work they do.

Being a police dog handler is a long-term commitment, looking after a dog's every need throughout its working life and into retirement. Dog handlers work shifts and can be called to any incident where a dog could assist. The handlers, with the help of their dogs, are responsible for the arrest of thousands of criminals annually.

SUMMARY OF THE SELECTION PROCESS

The selection process for a General Purpose Police Dog, usually a German or Belgian Shepherd (further specialist roles as a Trainer and Search Dog Handler comes from the expertise shown as a General Purpose Dog Handler) is normally done by way an application form, with the ability to answer all questions i.e. tick every box, followed by personal interview.

Once you have submitted your application form for the role of police dog handler it will be reviewed by a board of senior officers to determine the candidate's suitability for the position. If they do not feel the candidate is suitable, or has not demonstrated that they possess the qualities needed for the role, they will not proceed to the next stage.

The purpose of the recruitment process is for the assessors to find out as much as possible about a candidate's suitability for the role. From the candidate's perspective it is his or

her opportunity to present themselves in the best possible light.

THE POLICE DOG HANDLER APPLICATION FORM

The dog handler application form differs from the application form to become a police officer in a number of ways. Firstly, when you apply to become a police officer there is a standard application form that candidates must complete and submit which includes a number of core competencies. These core competency questions are designed to test your suitability to the role of police officer. If you can demonstrate that you possess these competencies then you will be asked to attend a national assessment centre.

When you apply for the role of a police dog handler you will have already been a serving officer for at least 2 years and completed your probationary period. At this point if you then want to specialise in the field of police dog handling you will need to complete an internal application form when a job arises.

The role of police dog handler is one of the most sought after career paths within the police force and you need to ensure that you submit a strong application form. The first step after you have completed your 2 year probation is to keep an eye out for dog handler jobs either on the jobs board, the intranet or your main police forces websites.

These types of jobs do not become available very often for the reason that those whom become dog handler tend to stay as serving dog handlers. So keeping an eye out for a position is a must, the last thing you want to do is miss the opportunity to apply for the post.

Another point to bear in mind is that not all police forces

have a dog section and therefore do not require dog handlers, they often bring them in from the larger forces if need be. Therefore you need to bear this in mind when applying to a particular police force.

Each Police Force within the UK will typically have a standard form for internal applicants looking to specialise or transfer that can then be applied to a number of roles. This application form will usually have set questions which can be applied to the particular position that has become available. These application forms vary from force to force.

The application form will normally be accompanied by guidance notes; you will not just receive the application form by itself. It is very important that you read these guidance notes as they refer to the job itself, the role and more importantly the application form you are about to fill out.

For example the guidance notes will typically contain a page entitled "What we expect from you". So many candidates ignore the guidance notes but you can pick up useful information about what they are looking for in a good response just by taking the time to read these notes.

If you are serious about becoming a dog handler then speak to the people involved in recruiting for your police force, ask them about the internal application form and see if you can obtain a copy. It is worth noting that more and more applications are now moving online but more often than not a paper copy will still be available.

If you can obtain an application form early then you can start to prepare your answers for role of police dog handler. The result is that when a position becomes available, it may only be available for a week before it is closed, but because you have obtained a copy early you have more time to prepare

a stronger application. This can help you gain an edge over the other applicants who only have a week to prepare.

The length of response that you provide for each question should be determined by the amount of space available to you on the application form or the specified number of words. The form itself may provide you with the facility to attach a separate sheet if necessary. If it doesn't then make sure you keep to the space provided.

The application form questions below are sample application questions that you may get asked on your application form. They are used for guidance purposes to enable you to create your own individual response. In the interview you may be asked to expand upon what you have written in your application form and if the answer does not relate to you then you could struggle to give a clear and concise response.

Top Tip

Before you send off your application form or submit your application form (if doing so online) ensure that you save a copy so that you read over your responses before attending the interview. Therefore if you are asked to expand upon the responses you have given they will be fresh in your mind.

- Why do you want to become a Police dog handler?

- Why would you make a good Police Dog handler?

- What do you think the role of a Police Dog handler entails?

- What are the qualities required for this role?

- What have you done so far to find out about the role of a dog handler?

- Do you own or have you ever owned a dog?

- Do you have any previous experience of dog handling? If so, please provide details.

- Give examples of when you have had to work as a team.

- Give examples of when you have had to work independently.

- What do you understand about the term equality and fairness?

- What do you understand by the term 'equal opportunities'?

WHAT THE BOARD OF SENIOR OFFICER'S CONSIDER WHEN DECIDING IF A CANDIDATE IS APPLICABLE

What do they look for from your 2 year probation period?

- As with any other specialist role within the Police, the 2 year probation period has to be completed. This is to satisfy the Service that you are a competent Officer for normal day to day work. It is from this period onwards that you have to prove you have the other specific attributes.

- A proven track record with an ability to work on your own (You may be the only other Dog Handler on duty within your Force area). Respond to any situation and take the appropriate action (From missing person to murder scene).

- You must have a mature attitude and able to account for your own decisions. In effect a good all round Police Officer and of course a reference from your immediate supervisory Officer indicating your suitability.

- A good knowledge of the law, particularly the powers of arrest and the use of force (an Officer can be guilty of assault if the Police Dog does not respond effectively to command i.e. does not release)

- Are there any outstanding 'disciplinary investigations' which could affect the application? This can be a deciding factor when considering a candidate for the role of police dog handler. Competition is tough for this job and you do not want to reduce your chances by appearing problematic.

- You will need a 'full motor car' driving licence (for patrol purposes) but hopefully you should already have that.

If you do not have a driving license then I would recommend that you take steps to begin the process of learning to drive and wait until you are a competent driver before applying for the role. Driving will be an essential part of a police dog handler's role as you will often be called to crime scenes when required by your fellow officers. In addition to this, you may also be required to work with smaller forces who do not have a dog unit and if you do not possess a driving licence your are limiting your ability to fit the job description.

- Why does the candidate want to be a dog handler?

The reasons behind the candidate wanting to become a police dog handler are an important consideration for the board of senior officers. At this point they will take into account the response on the application form including the candidate's motivation for applying for the role.

The key point here is that the dog should be a tool to assist the Officer and not something to hide behind. Aggression and the use of force should be the last resort of the team.

- Does the candidate have a natural affinity towards dog handling and is their any evidence of this?

- Does the candidate own or has ever owned a dog? Have they ever involved in dog training?

Maybe you already own your own dog and have attended dog training lessons and courses in the past. If so, try and include this in your application as once again the highlights your suitability to the role.

- Does the candidate even like dogs? As this cannot always be assumed

- If the candidate already owns a dog/s would the Police Dog be now one too many?

(Could the time, care and additional training be provided at home? The 'dog handler's allowance' pays for this additional care at home)

- Do they have any preference of breed or sex of the dog?

- What would they do if they were offered a dog they didn't like, for whatever reason? Could they handle the rearing of a puppy whilst continuing normal Police duties until the dog is accepted for formal training?

(Not all Forces have a breeding programme and can offer a puppy. It is normal for most Forces to accept and assess gift dogs from 18 months to 3 years old, which are then passed to the potential handler.)

- Does the candidate live in a property that can accommodate a dog?

Police Dogs live at home with the handler, normally in a purpose built outside kennel. Is the property enclosed? A Police Dog is a dangerous dog, under control. It is trained to bite and all risks should be avoided. A flat would be unsuitable.

- Being a Police Dog Handler is normally a commitment for about 7 years (the working life of one dog) and is the candidate willing to provide that commitment?

- Does the candidate's spouse/partner support this application?

- Initial dog training courses are for 13 weeks and make take the Officer away from home for that period. Would this cause a problem?

- A knowledge of the law relating to dogs i.e. Protection of Animals Act 1911, Dangerous Dogs Act 1991 etc

WHAT THEY LOOK FOR DURING THE SUITABILITY COURSE

Not all Forces run a suitability course, but may offer the candidate the opportunity to join handlers on 'day training exercises'. If this is the case with your force then you may be asked to spend the day with the dog school for the other dog handlers to assess your ability to fulfil this role.

- Overall a general fitness that would enable the handler to keep up with the dog's training i.e. tracking (the handler is required to make progress at the end of a 'tracking line' and not impede the dog), heelwork (intensive footwork by the handler at the side of the dog) and running (to get to the dog as soon as possible in the training of 'searching' and 'criminal work'.

- All candidates and handlers have to participate in 'criminal work training' i.e. at some stage allowing themselves to be bitten by a Police Dog (whilst wearing protective clothing, however accidents do sometimes happen!)

- Honesty by the candidate as to their own suitability.

POLICE DOG HANDLER INTERVIEW

- The interview panel will be made up of at least two

interviewers and prior to the interview you will be sent details / verbally informed of when and where the interview will take place.

- The interview panel will introduce themselves and one of them will welcome you, giving you an explanation of what will take place, i.e. that you will be asked a series of questions, some of which have a number of parts and that you can ask for any questions to be repeated.

- The interviewers will expect you to know what the role will of a police dog handler will involve and to have thought about what makes them the best person for the role.

- The questions you will be asked will be set standard questions, based around the job role that you are applying for. Each interviewee will be asked the same standard questions and they will be marking down the response you provide during the interview. This means that even if the interviewer is not looking at you they will be listening.

- You must sell yourself to the panel. You need to show the recruitment staff that you have the skills and abilities for the role of police dog handler within this police force.

Below is a list of sample questions with sample responses that you may be asked during the police dog handler interview process. As with the application form sample questions it is advisable to create your own unique answers that you are comfortable expanding upon should you be requested to do so.

You may also notice that the some of the application questions and interview questions overlap and this will often be the case. Try to provide a different answer to the one you gave on the application form.

The final stage of the Police dog handler selection process is the interview. Under normal circumstances the board will consist of up to 3 senior police officers. It is important to remember that whilst you will be nervous don't let this get in the way of your success. You are capable of becoming a Police dog handler and the nerves that you have on the day are only natural, in fact they will help you to perform better if you have prepared sufficiently.

As part of the interview process you may be questioned on the answers you have submitted on your application form, so always keep a backup and read through them before the interview to refresh your memory.

The purpose of the interview is for the assessors/interviewers to find out as much as possible about a candidate's suitability for the role. From the candidate's perspective it is his or her opportunity to present themselves in the best possible light.

The first step in preparing for the police dog handler interview is to undertake sufficient research. However, we do not mean research just for the sake of it. If you are going to spend time researching a role, then it needs to be focused and worthwhile. This guide is a great starting point in your research, but you should not stop there. You would probably find that talking and interacting with police dog handlers would be an effective method of researching, rather than spending hours reading articles or literature. This is as you can gain a good insight to what is required of a competent dog hander from them, and they will help you prepare for any questions asked on interview.

Of course not everybody can predict the type of questions you will be asked at the interview, but they will be structured around the role and your **personal qualities** and

experiences. Therefore the more you know about the position you are applying for the better prepared you will be.

YOUR INTRODUCTION

You may be given the opportunity to tell the panel about yourself, or the interviewer may go straight into asking you questions that are relevant to the role. You should prepare a response beforehand in case you are asked "to introduce yourself to the panel" or "tell us about yourself", the last thing you want to do is be lost for words. If you have previously thought about what you are going to say it will come more naturally to you in the interview environment.

These are common questions that many interviewers use to break the ice. A big mistake usually made by the majority of people is that they focus on their family, children, hobbies or home life. Avoid these, unless specifically asked and try to base your answer on personal achievements, educational background and ongoing studies.

You can use the introduction as an opportunity to sell yourself. You should cover brief topics relating to your experience, qualifications, outside interests and ambitions. If you tell the panel that in your spare time you are working towards a qualification that can relate to the role you are applying for then this can only be a good thing. Try to keep your introduction as brief as possible and don't go over 2 minutes in length.

Q. First and foremost, why does the candidate want to be a dog handler?

Sample Response:

"To enhance my abilities by utilising those of a well trained

Police Dog to assist my colleagues in their duties. From finding a lost child to protecting the innocent from the most violent and from searching for lost property to finding the hidden criminal. Be prepared to further expand on the value of a Police Dog".

THINGS TO CONSIDER:

Have you ever seen a Police dog in action during your years as a serving officer, were you impressed? If so, why?

Include this in your response to give a personal and honest reason for wanting to become a dog handler.

Maybe it was the way the dog handler used their skills to control and diffuse a situation that was becoming out of control or maybe it was the way the handler and the dog worked together to apprehend a suspect who was hiding.

Q. Do you have a natural affinity towards dog handling and do you have any evidence of this? Do you own or have you ever owned a dog?

Sample Response:

"I have grown up amongst dog owning families and have always enjoyed their company and affection. I have owned/ handled a dog for***** number of years and feel that this has provided me with an good understanding of dog handling which I can transfer to this role."

Q. Have you ever been involved in dog training?

Sample Response:

"I have attended dog training classes and attained ********. I have always been willing to learn new techniques and would be a complete novice in Police Dog training."

 how2become

It is unlikely that at this point you have ever attended any police dog training courses however if you have attended training classes or courses with your own dog/s then it is worth mentioning at this point as it will demonstrate a willingness to learn and develop.

Q. If the candidate already owns a dog/s would the Police Dog be now one too many?

Sample Response:

"No the police Dog would become another member of the family, not a pack, and would receive all the necessary attention it requires. I would be fully committed to ensuring that police dog fitted in without any problems."

Q. Being a Police Dog Handler is normally a commitment for about 7 years (the working life of one dog) and is the candidate willing to provide that commitment?

Sample Response:

"I am more than willing to provide that commitment and have considered this thoroughly before making the decision to apply for this post. I am also aware and fully understand that upon reaching the conclusion of the 7 years service the police dog will retire and generally with the handler. I am willing to make this commitment to both myself and the police dog".

Q. Does your spouse/partner support your application?

Sample Response:

"I recognise that becoming a dog handler is a full time commitment to make both in terms of training and caring for the dog. In preparation for this role time has been spent discussing this issue and all of its implications and I have full support of my partner in this decision".

Q. Initial dog training courses are for 13 weeks and make take the Officer away from home for that period. Would this cause a problem?

"The fact that I may be away for 13 weeks does not cause any foreseeable problems at this time and once more this has been fully discussed with those most affected."

Further interview questions:

Q. Why do you want to become a Police dog handler?

Q. Why would you make a good Police Dog handler?

Q. What do you think the role of a Police Dog handler entails?

Q. What are the qualities required to become a dog handler

Q. What have you done so far to find out about the role of a dog handler?

Please note that these questions may be similar to the ones asked on your application form. The key here is not to just repeat the answer that you provided on your application form but to either expand on it or provide a different example.

KEY: While your are likely to be asked more common questions such as "why do you want to become a police dog handler" you may also be required to *provide examples* of when you have demonstrated certain competencies during your years as a serving officer. In preparation for these types of questions try to think of examples during your years as an officer when you have **demonstrated:**

- Teamwork

- Personal responsibility

- Problem Solving

- Effective Communication

- Community and Customer Focus

- Resilience

For example, you may be asked to provide an example of when you have to work effectively as a team to reach a common goal, what was the outcome and what role did you play in helping the team achieve this goal?

TIP

Use the STAR model when giving examples to answers you have been asked:

- Describe the **S**ituation

- Describe the **T**ask

- Describe the **A**ction

- Describe the **R**esult

If you already have an example in mind because you have prepared effectively you will be able to recall your answer during the interview. On the other hand if you have to think about an example right there and then you may find your mind goes blank under the pressure.

These types of competency based questions will be similar to the questions that you were asked when you first joined the police force. However, the difference is that now you will be expected to provide examples from your serving years as an officer whereas previously your examples would have been drawn from other jobs or life experiences.

More general types of questions you could be asked:
Q. What are your strengths and what could you being to the role?

When answering this type of question we would advise that you give work related examples. You should try to think of 3 good strengths that you possess and try to give an example of when you have used those strengths. You must demonstrate to the panel that you are able to prove your strengths as opposed to just saying that you have them. Anyone can say that they are motivated, enthusiastic, dedicated or reliable but proving that you have those strengths is a different matter. Being able to demonstrate that you have strengths will give you higher scores.

Q. What is your greatest weakness

Possibly the worst answer you can give for a question of this nature is that you don't have any weaknesses. Being able to identify that you have weaknesses is a strength in itself and you should have at least 2 weaknesses that you can explain. Obviously it is important that you answer this question carefully as you could reduce your chances of success if you sell yourself in a negative light.

Possibly a good example to use is as follows:

Your response should identify that you have a weakness but also identifies a number of strengths. It should show you that you have the ability to look at yourself and make changes where needed. Accepting constructive criticism is one thing but doing something about it is another. This also leads on to another possible 'Strength' quality in the fact that you have the strength to identify your weaknesses and do something about them!

Should you ask questions at the end of the interview?
This is a time for you to ask some questions to the panel. You should usually have 2 or 3 questions that you want to ask at the end. Make sure they are relevant but avoid asking questions relating to leave or salary (unless you are asked).

Ask specific questions that relate to the role or development opportunities within the organisation. Don't ask questions where you are trying to be clever or questions that are too technical. If you try to catch them out they won't be impressed and they may come back and ask you a similar one.

THE END OF THE INTERVIEW

Make sure you remain positive at this stage and thank the entire panel for their time. This is even a good opportunity to shake their hands.

A list of don'ts for the interview:

- Do not turn up later for the interview – ensure you leave in plenty of time. If you are not sure where the location of the interview is being held find out the day before

- Do not ramble or waffle when providing a response to an interview question. If you do not know the answer to the question, pause for a minute and take the time to think about your response before providing an answer

- Do not provide short or one word answers – you will be expected to expand upon an answer and more often than not provide an example.

- Do not go off on a tangent – remember to stay focused on the question you have been asked and answer it clearly and concisely.

- Do not sit with your arms folded or allow yourself to slouch down in the chair – sit up right with your hands on your lap.

- Do not use slang or words such as "Er…" or make noises such as "mmm…" while you and trying to think of your

response. If you need time to think remain silent while you do so.

- If you are transferring from another force do not make unnecessary and derogatory comments about current employers. If asked about why you want to chance forces focus on the positive aspects of the new job as opposed to any negative aspects of your current job. This can show a lack of professionalism.

- Finally, do not allow nervous factors or indicators to take over such as fidgeting or cracking knuckles, try to appear confident in yourself and the answers you provide.

TOP INSIDER HINTS & TIPS TO HELP YOU BECOME A POLICE DOG HANDLER

TIP I

Make yourself known to the Dog Section and show your interest prior to any vacancies being posted.

This is very important and something under estimate by a lot of candidates. By making yourself known you are expressing an interest in this role at an early stage. In addition to this, you will get to know the people within the dog handling unit and discover a higher level of understanding about the role and what is required. This knowledge can then be expressed in the application form and interview stage.

TIP 2

Ask if you can visit and participate in training, in your own time. A great way to significantly increase you chances of becoming a police dog handler is to provide evidence to the board that you are drawn towards dog handling and that this is something of interest to you outside work.

Spend some time with the dog handling unit in your police force (if your force does not have a dog handling unit find the nearest one to you), get to know the dog handlers and show an interest in dog handling even if this means putting in a few extras in or coming in on your dog off.

By making this type of commitment you will be showing the senior officers that you are serious about this role and committed enough to investing your own time to discover more. You will then put yourself above all the other candidates who have not made this extra commitment.

TIP 3

Be willing to listen and learn, Police Dog trainers like a blank sheet to work on, with no pre-conceived ideas and definitely in the 'initial' contact stages 'no arguing.'

TIP 4

Keep a good standard of fitness as a vacancy may appear at any time.

A good insight to what is required of a competent dog hander will be gleaned from the handlers themselves and prepare you for any questions asked on interview.

TIP 5

As with most job interviews, research the history of the Police Dog, both locally and nationally and have some knowledge of the animal itself, the dog. This does not have to be to Veterinary standard, but of things that assist in everyday care (this can be obtained from this guide)

TIP 6

Even if a question has been asked by one interviewer you should not focus on that interviewer when answering as

this may exclude the other interviewer/s. You should aim to make eye contact with both interviewers when answering a question.

JOB RELATED FITNESS TEST

As you will be aware, policing requires you to handle a variety of situations involving physically challenging tasks, calling for a certain level of endurance and strength. The Job Related Fitness Test (JRFT) is designed to assess these aspects of your fitness.

DYNAMIC STRENGTH

Your dynamic strength represents your ability to exert muscular force continuously over time, to perform tasks such as lifting, carrying, pushing and pulling, without suffering the onset of early fatigue. The JRFT uses a device called a Dyno machine to test your dynamic strength. You will be required to push 34kgs and pull 35kgs.

After carefully positioning you on the Dyno, an assessor will ask you to perform three gentle seated chest pushes as a warm up.

They will then ask you to push five times using maximum effort, with only three seconds of recovery time between each effort. Once you have completed this pushing exercise, the assessor will position you at the opposite end with your chest pushed against the padding. As with the pushing test, after three gentle warm-ups you will be asked to perform five pulls at maximum effort.

ENDURANCE

Your level of endurance is your ability to continue physically

exerting yourself over time – i.e. how long you can 'keep going'. The JRFT tests your endurance by requiring you to reach level 5.4, which relates to 4 shuttles at level 5. This involves continuous running for approximately 3 minutes and 30 seconds to and fro along a 15-metre track in time with a series of bleeps. The timing between bleeps is slow at first, but becomes gradually progressively faster as the test goes on, requiring you to increase your work rate and speed. The test will end when you can no longer keep up with the bleeps.

You do not have to be an Olympic athlete to successfully complete the JRFT! We are interested only in whether you meet the minimum standard of fitness required to operate effectively as a Police Officer. If you prepare yourself properly, there is no reason for you to fail. Please be aware that for certain specialist roles i.e. Firearms, you may be required to achieve a higher level of the medical and fitness test. However, even if you don't pass at your first attempt, you will be allowed to re-take within an agreed time span. If you fail after three attempts your application will be unsuccessful and you will not be eligible to re-apply for six months.

FURTHER CAREER OPTIONS: POLICE DOG TRAINERS

Sometimes Police Dog Handlers may wish to become trainers themselves, or there may be a dog trainer who would like to become a police dog trainer. As an example of a position for a police dog trainer with Hampshire Constabulary, the role profile states that the Constabulary has 65 dogs in its Dog Section which are based all over the county. The dogs are housed at the homes of either a Handler or a Trainer and they work from their local police station. All Police Dog Handlers are serving Police Officers.

The Constabulary states that the main function of their Police Dog Trainers is to design, plan and carry out all initial and continuation training for police dogs and their handlers. The Trainers also assess and monitor potential police dogs for the force. This involves liaising with dog breeders, rescue homes, dog training classes, etc., to procure potential police dogs and to undertake the assessment of potential dogs, including maintaining dogs at home where appropriate.

To become a Dog Trainer, a candidate needs to have previous experience in providing training relevant to police dog requirements, i.e., tracking, searching and protection work, along with experience in the initial stages of dog training, i.e., puppies and young dogs. As a Trainer, a candidate will be expected to have knowledge and experience of researching and designing training programmes, therefore needing effective communication skills, both verbal and written, leadership and motivational skills, along with the ability to work as part of a team.

CHAPTER 8
POLICE DOG TRAINING COURSES

INTRODUCTION

The training of police dogs and police dog handlers is an individualised process. Each dog has its own character and temperament and each handler must learn his or her dog's every like and dislike, action and reaction to whatever may happen to the dog, or indeed to the handler. The handler needs to be able to anticipate what the dog might do next in any given situation. Therefore it's of paramount importance that the handler not only knows the dog, but that he is knowledgeable about dogs and their behaviour. Diligent study and a lot of hard work and patience are the best way for a handler to learn how to train a dog.

CONTROL

Control of the dog is important, but so is self-control for

the handler. If a handler loses his temper easily, he will lose control of the dog. Training demands patience and repetition and the handler will be rewarded for his self-control by a dog which is devoted, learns more quickly and is eager to please. The handler's attitude to training is vital, and both dog and handler should look forward to training sessions, not dread them. Dogs love to please their master, but it's easy to break a dog's spirit so it will obey, but without joy. The goal is to train a dog to obey commands by learning the correct response and being rewarded for it every time.

Training a dog to obey a command takes time. The dog needs to learn first of all that it cannot ignore a command and it cannot escape the fact that the handler expects obedience. The handler also needs to realise that if his dog does not obey or complete the command, it may not have yet learned what is required of it. Association between the command and the action it is being asked to do must be made by the dog before the sequence of command and action is learned. This learning process can take time, according to the dog's temperament and character, but the dog must keep learning for as long as it takes for each single command and action to become second nature to the dog. The handler, too, needs to realise that he needs to stay with one command and action until the dog has learned it, before moving on to teach the dog how to respond to a new command.

The handler must be firm with the dog, so that the dog learns that each time a command is given, the handler expects it to carry out the action. In this way, an excellent and reliable working team is created.

Control of the dog is at first undertaken by the lead, which is a very important tool when training. The handler uses the lead to encourage the dog to move in a certain way or to

cease a movement. The lead should never be jerked, but used with a constant pressure when directing the dog. When the dog has learned to carry out a command correctly on the lead, then the handler's voice and visual actions – which are earlier combined with the lead work – should be enough for the dog to understand and command and to obey.

ASSOCIATION

Dogs work by association – they learn to link actions with areas or people or situations. Therefore training should be greatly varied in where it takes place and the activities played out in areas that the dog cannot associate with any one place. Familiarity with training in one action in one area may lead to the dog anticipating an action even before the command is given.

However, the police dog needs to react to each command in the same way every time, no matter the location. The handler must keep his voice consistent in tone and attitude in order not to confuse the dog. Also, he must keep in mind that his visual commands need to be consistent so that the dog has no doubt as to what is required of it.

REPETITION

Dogs get bored as easily as human beings. Therefore, the repetition of a command-action exercise can be overdone and lead to boredom for the dog as well as its handler. However, repetition is the only way that a dog can learn to associate the words of the handler with the action he is asking it to do. As mentioned before, dogs love to please their master, so they have a desire to keep on trying to do what they're being asked to do and will continue until they are clearly bored. Control of the dog then becomes an issue.

In order to train a police dog to obey on command with immediate response, it is necessary to use repetition of voice, action and reward or correction until it is clear the dog understands. From the very beginning of training, a dog must be corrected if it takes up a wrong stance or if it does not obey. Correction, not punishment, is the only way to train a dog in the early stages. If boredom does begin to show, it's okay to move on to a new exercise briefly, or one that has already been learned. It's even better to allow the dog to play for a while, as boredom can make a dog unhappy. The understanding of his dog's character and boredom levels makes it easier for the handler to continue with the repetitive nature of learning.

COMMANDS

Repetition of a command, once given by the handler, does not ensure that the dog will carry out the command. A dog can be confused if a command is repeated. When a dog learns what is expected of him by the handler's command, the dog will do its best to obey. If there is a variation in the handler's voice or in the way a command is given, this will also confuse the dog. It's usually better to give a command in a quiet voice so that the dog will listen more intently.

If the handler gives a wrong command, the dog must be allowed to carry out that command, even if it is not what the handler intended, before the correct command is then given to the dog. Whenever a dog completes a command correctly, the handler should reward the dog with praise. Commands should be short words, delivered clearly and with confidence, but not loudly. The dog learns to respond to the handler's tone of voice and will eventually associate the command given with the action required.

REWARDS

Rewarding a dog for carrying out a command correctly is an important part of its training. Even human beings respond to rewards for their efforts, so how much more does a faithful animal learn to act as its handler commands, in order to receive that longed-for praise from him. When a handler gives a command that the dog understands and connects with a correct action, on successful completion of that command, the handler should reward the dog. The handler will know what spurs his dog on to obedience and what the dog loves most, and he will provide that reward to honour the dog's obedience.

Some dogs just love a pat on the head and a fuss made of them, while others prefer a treat of food or a short play with their favourite toy. There is no shortcut to a dog's continued obedience – a reward every time is what will make that happen. Every successful completion of a task should bring a word of praise for the dog. A dog soon learns to recognise those words and the tone of voice as well and looks forward to them. Not praising a dog's obedience will not make a happy dog.

If a dog is having trouble learning to carry out a certain command correctly, after a short period of play, the handler should move on to an exercise that the dog has learned. That obedience should be rewarded with praise and a physical reward, so that the training session ends happily. A dog does not want to be left with a sense of having failed to please its trainer. Success and rewards make for a good team.

CORRECTION

Dogs are a little like young children, in that they learn by

praise and correction. Withholding praise is usually sufficient to teach a dog that its handler is not happy, unlike children, who can understand much easier what is being asked of them and who can learn right from wrong. Dogs do not have these standards, so they must learn by a system of rewards and correction. However, as with children, dogs should not be corrected by someone who has lost their temper, as this only creates fear as well as confusion. Sometimes the simple word 'no' will bring the dog to the point of realising that its handler is requiring something more than what it's just done.

As has been said, each dog is different and has its own temperament, so the handler needs to know what type of correction will suit his dog and bring it back into line. The correction also depends on what the dog has done that is not correct, in order for the connection to be made in the dog's mind. It's not helpful to correct a dog for an old mistake, as this will only confuse it. As soon as the dog behaves incorrectly, the handler must correct the dog, so letting it know that something is not right.

A dog should never be corrected for being slow in learning. Each dog is different in its ability to learn and to make associations. Some dogs are over eager and must be corrected because they are too intent on carrying out any task in order to please. Even if a dog is slow in executing a command, when the dog has completed it correctly, the handler must praise it, however long it took. Handlers should only correct dogs when a command is not carried out properly.

When the dog is being trained on the lead at the beginning of the training course, the handler should never use the lead to reprimand the dog. The lead is used as a tool to help the dog complete the correct movements or stance when it is learning, together with the verbal command. This is the same with

physical touch by the handler. When a dog needs help in learning to 'sit' or other positions, the handler's contact with the dog should be firm and consistent, but never hurtful to the dog. Hitting a dog will never bring about obedience, but will only serve to make the dog resentful or frightened. A dog should come to regard its handler's hands as reassuring and a welcome sign of affection and praise.

As correction is part of the process of learning, consistent repetition is important for the dog to understand what is required and what it not allowed. The dog's handler must also learn to use correction as a tool to bring about the end result of a successful working team. The handler must, however, take due care never to be cruel to his dog during training nor on the job, as he is legally accountable by the Protection of Animals Act 1911. The law states that any correction must be necessary and reasonable, only using approved equipment (such as the lead for guidance) if needed.

TRAINING COURSES

There are a variety of training courses for the different types of dogs used by police forces around the country, to enable specific training to fit the dogs and to provide this form of law enforcement where it is needed. The main courses are reviewed below.

CLASSROOM WORK

Handlers and dogs do not only train practically in exercises and obedience to command scenarios. There is also a lot of hard work that takes place in classrooms for the handler to learn the theory of dog handling and all that it involves. Whereas practical work with the dog is taught

under individual instruction, the theory classroom work is done in groups.

Lectures

Qualified instructors will ensure handlers receive necessary information on the following:

- An introduction to training and the principles of training

- The care of a dog, its grooming and how to examine it

- How to feed a dog and ensure its hygiene

- What equipment is required, how to care for it and use it

- The basic anatomy of dogs

- First aid for dogs

- The theory of tracking, scent and searching

- The operational use of police dogs

- The law relating to dogs

- The value of continuation and refresher courses

- The maintenance of standards

These subjects all have several sections with very technical learning. The handler must learn all about scent – both how a dog scents and how it distinguishes different scents – and also the things that can affect scent. This is an important subject because so much replies on the dog's ability to detect and follow scents in its work.

The handler learns how to lay a track for the dog to learn to follow, all on different surfaces and terrains and in all types of weather conditions.

There is a lot to learn about the work of searching, either

for persons out in the open or within closes structures, for criminal suspects or for lost children. The search for objects such as cash, illegal substances, or explosives is another area that is covered in the classroom.

Criminal work opens a whole array of things to be learned and followed, beginning, as with all the areas of police work, with the Human Rights Act. Even criminals have rights and the dog police handler must learn these and adhere to them while trying to catch the criminal, using only necessary and legal force in doing so. The dog has to learn to chase and detain, chase and stand off, chase and hold, chase and attack and how to escort prisoners. The handler must also teach the dog how to face a test of courage against any weapon the criminal may raise against it when he is faced with a barking dog.

For each of the specialised areas, such as drugs search dogs, human remains search dogs, tactical firearms support dogs and explosives search dogs, the handler must also put in the bookwork in order to train the dog in the practical work.

Lectures are not one-sided, as there is ample opportunity to ask question and to discuss points between handlers and the tutor.

GENERAL PURPOSE INITIAL TRAINING COURSE

The training course for handlers who are just beginning will last anywhere from 10 to 12 weeks. Everyone must first complete an 8-week basic skills course at an approved police dog training centre under an Association of Chief Police Officers (ACPO) instructor. The handler must then successfully complete a further course on operational skills, lasting between 2 to 6 weeks.

Those handlers who are experienced with dogs also undertake a basic skills course, of up to 8 weeks.

All handlers must complete the requirements set, but some may have to undergo further training before they can go onto the field.

Aims

Each course begins with General Purpose Police Dog Training, for although some dogs will specialise in their particular type of police work, all dogs must learn from the beginning the specific commands and tasks to be carried out by all police dogs. All handlers must also learn to handle a general purpose police dog. All parts of the course must meet the ACPO requirements.

Successful completion of the course will enable the handler and his or her dog to be competent in general obedience, agility, tracking, searching and criminal work. These are the requirements of the ACPO Unit of Assessment which must be fulfilled before the team can be operational on the job. The handler and the dog are assessed throughout the course.

Objectives

Both the handler and the dog are trained on the course, being assessed both individually and together. Their performance as a working team is of utmost importance for the course to be completed and passed.

The objectives of the course for the police dog handler are as follows:

- To learn the correct use of the dog lead and harness or collar chain

- To be able to use the correct verbal and visual commands

- To use the agility equipment correctly

- To learn the methods for searching areas and properties and apply them in the correct way

- To learn how to search buildings

- To correctly pursue and detain criminal suspects

- To be able to use the police dog correctly in aggressive situations

- To enable the handler to progress to operation under control and perhaps with guidance.

For the police dog's training, the following are necessary:

- For the dog to be able to respond correctly to command

- To obey command to a competent standard

- To be able to track a person over any environment

- To find articles dropped on a track

- To search for missing people or suspects and indicate their find

- To search within buildings for people or property

- To locate stolen or lost property

- To chase suspects and detain them

- To chase suspects and keep them secured until the handler arrives

- To assist in controlling a disorderly crowd or person

- To be controlled in behaviour whenever in a work situation.

Health and Safety
Once again, both the handler and the dog must learn and pass the Health and Safety regulations.

The handler must learn the correct use of the protective equipment used in training his or her dog. He must also learn the legislation on dangerous dogs and the correct use of equipment use to capture or detain dangerous dogs he may come in contact with in his work.

The handler must prove his understanding, ability and willingness to look after his dog and its physical, mental and emotional needs, so that the dog is safe with him in his work and is also provided for in a healthy environment.

At the conclusion of the general purpose course, the handler will confidently instruct the dog to carry out the following commands:

- Obedience Exercises

  Heelwork
  Distance control
  Agility
  Recall
  Send away and redirect

- Criminal Work

  Straight chase
  Chase and stand off
  Emergency recall
  Stick and gun attack
  Crowd control

- Searching

  Location and indication of open and hidden people
  Property search with passive indication

- Tracking

  Pattern and practical tracks, and introduction to hard surface tracks and cross tracks.

The Assessor:

The assessor will be a serving police officer or an instructor employed by a police authority and the holder of an ACPO Instructors certificate.

Assessment methods:

1. Written exam on the theoretical content of the ACPO Training and Care Manual

2. Observation of the performance of the dog handler and police dog on simulated exercises in different environments.

3. With regards to the observation part of the assessment will be assessed on your ability to control and command the dog. Each exercise that you undertake you will be graded by your level of competency, which means that you are either competent or not competent. It is essential a pass or fail scoring system.

Exercises:

• HEELWORK

The handler can demonstrate complete control over the dog when walking to the heel

How you will be scored:

1. The dog will respond correct when being called to heel by the handler, with its right shoulder close to the knee of the handler

2. The handler demonstrate correct use of the lead and correction collar

3. The handler will be required to perform the exercises to include stand, sit and down.

4. The trainers ability to use visual and verbal commands to correct any mistake by the dog

5. The exercise will be performed to the required standard

- **RETRIEVE**

The dog must be able to retrieve any object when directed to do so by the handler.

How you will be scored:

1. The dog correctly follows the handler command

2. Control of the dog is maintained by the handler at all times

3. The handler competently uses training commands to direct the dog

4. The dog must go forward, retrieve the object and return to the handler

- **DOWN – Handler out of Sight**

The dog must remain in the down position once the handler has disappeared out of sight

How you will be scored

1. The dog responds correctly to the handlers command

2. The handler demonstrates control of the dog

3. The trainer uses commands correctly

4. The dog stays in the down position until handler returns

• **DISTANCE CONTROL**

The handler can control the dog from a distance including being able to execute the following commands: sit, down and stand.

How you will be scored:

    1. The handler maintains control of the dog

    2. The dog performs the commands when instructed

• **SPEAK ON COMMAND**

Under direction from the handler the dog will be barking when directed to do so and stop barking when further directed by the handler.

How you will be scored:

    1. The dog will start barking when they are given the command by the handler

    2. The handler maintains in control of the dog at all times

    3. The hander is able to use both verbal and visual training commands

    4. The dog stops barking when directed to do so

• **STOPPING THE DOG**

The dog will be required to stop when directed by the handler. This command will be tested in a variety of different scenarios.

How you will be scored:

    1. The responds in the correct way to the handlers commands

2. The handler remains in control at all times

3. The handler is capable of using visual and verbal commands

• RECALL

The dog must return to the handler immediately when given the command by the handler.

How you will be scored:

1. The dog returns to the handler when called

2. The handler is in control at all times

3. The handler is capable of using visual and verbal commands

• SEND AWAY AND RE-DIRECTION

The handler must be able to send away the dog and the re-direct on command.

How you will be scored:

1. The dog must move to the directed point by the handler and remain there

2. The dog will then be re-directed to another point where it will remain until re-called by the handler

3. The handler is in control at all times

4. The handler is capable of using visual and verbal commands

• AGILITY – OBSTACLE

The dog must complete a 3 foot obstacle jump safely when under direction of the handler

How you will be scored:

1. The dog will jump the obstacle when directed by the owner

2. The dog will then remain stationary until joined by the owner

3. The handler is in control at all times

- **AGILITY 6 FOOT SCALE JUMP**

The dog handler must demonstrate that the dog is capable of completing the scale jump successfully.

How you will be scored:

1. The dog will successfully negotiate the scale jump

2. Once the task is completed the dog will remain stationary until they are re-called by the handler

3. The handler remains in control of the dog at all times

4. The dog responds correctly to the commands of the handler

- **AGILITY 9 FOOT LONG JUMP**

The dog handler must demonstrate that the dog is capable of completing the long jump successfully and safely.

How you will be scored:

1. The dog will successfully clear the obstacle

2. Once the task is completed the dog will remain stationary until joined by the hander

3. The handler remains in control of the dog at all times

4. The dog responds correctly to the commands of the handler

- **CRIMINAL WORK – chase and detain**

The dog will be required to chase a running person and detain them by seizing their right arm.

How you will be scored:

1. The dog will chase the runner on command of the handler

2. The dog will seize the right of in a firm manner until directed by the handler to leave

3. The dog will be called out by the handler and after searching the person the dog and the handler will carry out an escort

4. The handler remains in control of the dog at all times

5. The dog responds correctly to the commands of the handler

- **CRIMINAL WORK – chase and stand off**

The dog is required to chase after a running person, the running person will stop when the dog approaches and the dog is required to stand off and detain the person.

How you will be scored:

1. The dog will chase after the runner when instructed by the handler

2. When the running person stops the dog will stand off and prevent the runner from leaving

3. The dog will then be called out when the handler arrives on the scene

4. The handler remains in control of the dog at all times

5. The dog responds correctly to the commands of the handler

- **CRIMINAL WORK – stick attack**

The dog will be required to attack a criminal who is armed with a stick.

How you will be scored:

1. When given the command by the handler the dog will chase the runner

2. The dog will take a firm hold of the runners right arm until instructed to leave by the handler

3. The handler will disarm the runner and command the dog to leave

4. The handler remains in control of the dog at all times

5. The dog responds correctly to the commands of the handler

- **CRIMINAL WORK – gun attack**

The dog will be required to attack a criminal who is armed with a gun

How you will be scored:

1. When given the command by the handler the dog will chase the runner

2. The dog will take a firm hold of the runners right arm until instructed to leave by the handler

3. The handler will disarm the runner and command the dog to leave

4. The handler remains in control of the dog at all times

5. The dog responds correctly to the commands of the handler

- **CRIMINAL WORK – Crowd control**

The dog must demonstrate the ability to deal effectively with aggressive and non aggressive crowds.

How you will be scored:

1. When confronted with a non aggressive crowd the dog must demonstrate a clam temperament

2. The dog will deal effectively when faced with an aggressive crowd

3. The handler should demonstrate an understanding of how dogs should be used in crowd situations

4. The handler remains in control of the dog at all times

5. The dog responds correctly to the commands of the handler

- **CRIMINAL WORK – Attack on Handler**

The dog must attack a criminal who attacks either the handler or the dog themselves.

How you will be scored:

1. The dog will 'unhesitatingly' defend either themselves or the handler when under attack

2. The dog will take a firm hold of the runners right arm until instructed to leave by the handler

- **TRACKING**

The dog will be required to undertake a tracking exercise over various terrains.

How you will be scored:

1. The handler will demonstrate the correct use of the tracking harness and line

2. The dog will accurately follow a track of human scent and indicate the presence of objects left along the track

- **SEARCHING PROPERTY**

The dog is required to enter the property and search the area and indicate to the dog handler the presence of a number of objects

How you will be scored:

1. The dog must indicate the presence of objects within the search area

2. The handler must use the dog in an effective manner to conduct the search of the area

3. The handler must demonstrate a thorough search technique

4. The handler remains in control of the dog at all times

5. The dog responds correctly to the commands of the handler

- **SEARCHING PERSONS**

The dog is required to undertake the search of a building and open area to locate the person and once located the dog will alert the owner by barking

How you will be scored:

1. The dog must search the area, locate the person and then indicate their presence within the search area by barking

2. The handler must use the dog in an effective manner to conduct the search of the area

3. The handler must demonstrate a thorough search technique

4. The handler remains in control of the dog at all times

5. The dog responds correctly to the commands of the handler

REFRESHER COURSE – GENERAL PURPOSE

This course varies with local police stations and requirements for that particular area, but usually lasts for 10 days every year.

Aims

This refresher course helps handlers to be reminded of basic training and also gives an opportunity to improve their handling of their dog. It also allows the team of handler and dog to be assessed as to their annual progress. There are usually work situations used for training, which includes night incidents.

Objectives

Once again, the ACPO Unit of Assessment is used to mark the general standard of the handler and the dog.

The refresher course helps to build on basic training and also give further instruction by giving the opportunity to correct general obedience faults that may have occurred in the working environment. It also helps to ensure that the handler is applying his commands correctly. If the handler is using any of the working equipment, such as the tracking harness and line, incorrectly, this can be corrected during the

refresher course. The handler and dog team's search procedures will be assessed and corrected if not carried out properly. They will be tested on the proper use of the dog in aggressive situations and in the chase and detain procedure.

The dog will have the opportunity in refresher training to prove its correct response to its handler's commands and, if there is room for improvement, to work on the standard of obedience. Tracking skills will be advanced on all surfaces and any faults in indicating articles will be corrected. Standards of search and criminal work will be assessed and improved.

DRUG DETECTION DOG – INITIAL COURSE

Certain dogs have the better skills at drug detection, and although they will have also attained the necessary level of obedience to command and control through general training, they will also need to be trained at the specialised work of drug detection.

This 6-week course is designed hone the dog's natural abilities of scent and awareness and to train the handler to handle the dog correctly in this specialised work. The handler will need special tuition in order to learn to recognise his dog's every expression and movement, while the dog is trained to detect the required controlled substances.

After the specialised drug training, the handler and dog also complete the operational based training as on a general purpose course.

Aims
Drugs enforcement is a growing problem for every police force, so there is a demand for detection of drugs in all situations of the trade and in most areas.

Objectives

The course is designed to ensure the ability of the handler to control his dog for a drug search. He or she needs to be self-motivated and conscientious and able to work without supervision. Common sense and confidence, determination and patience are definitely needed, as this work involves a lot of waiting and attention to the dog in public places, as well being in the public eye. It is not an easy job, but one that requires exact and close teamwork between the dog and the handler, as a missed opportunity to detect controlled substances can lead to bigger problems.

The dog should have the necessary search skills developed to a high level and it should be willing to work hard. It cannot be aggressive or nervous, but needs a good temperament, being capable to work in all conditions in for long periods of time. An ability to concentrate on the job at hand is imperative.

The handler must learn exactly how to work with a drug search dog and the correct way to work during a search. He must also be able to identify drugs and handle them safely, together with any accessories for using the drugs found with them.

The dog needs to be obedient whether working on or off the lead. It must be able to detect and indicate the presence of drugs in accordance with its training. The dog has to search in all areas, buildings, vehicles and outdoors in all conditions. The ability of the dog to ignore distractions such as noisy, constantly moving crowds, smells other than the drugs it is searching for and physical interference is of great importance. The training course ensures that the dog learns to become aware of the variety of environments it will be working in.

DRUG DETECTION – REFRESHER COURSE

This course usually is set for 10 days every year, in accordance with each Constabulary's needs.

Aims
It provides the opportunity for the team of handler and dog to ensure their detection work is in order and works well. The dog can also learn to detect a greater range of drugs, if necessary.

Objectives
The handler can prove his ability to search the necessary environments and the dog shows its competence in detecting drugs in all locations for its own patch.

The objective for the refresher is to ensure that the handler regularly encourages his dog in training with practice searches with positive finds. He should also be introducing the dog to varieties of the drugs the dog is familiar with.

The course gives the opportunity for the handler to update himself on the drug scene and methods of concealment and trends of use. He can also review problems he and his dog have faced and work through possible solutions for future situations.

TACTICAL FIREARMS SUPPORT DOG – INITIAL COURSE

This is usually a 4-week course.

Aims
Dogs and handlers are specially trained through this course to act as support for Tactical Firearms teams. The ACPO Manual of Guidance on Police Use of Firearms recommends that police dogs be used in all firearms operations.

Objectives

As a follow-on from basic training, the handler on this course will learn the correct use of specialised equipment, together with the verbal and visual commands needed for his canine co-worker. He will also need to be aware of the verbal and visual commands used by the Tactical Firearms Team and the methods of search they use so that he and his dog can closely support them during the search. The handler will learn how to use his dog in a close support role through the following situations:

- A building breach

- A prisoner retrieval

- In a stair and landing clearance

- In a loft clearance

- In a chase and detain of offenders situation

- To indicate 'line of flight' of an offender

- In the use of specialised equipment.

He will also learn the description and capabilities of various firearms.

During this course the police dog will be trained to respond correctly to its handler's commands. The handler must learn to help the dog respond to this additional role and also to tell the difference between a normal search command and execution of that command and the specialised commands and tasks of this role. The dog must be trained to carry out its systematic search under control and in the presence of other officers with weapons. It also must learn to act in support of officers with specialised equipment, such as respirators, and the dog must get used to gunfire and the possibility

of CS gas. The dog needs to learn to help escort a prisoner under its handler's control and accept different means of transportation.

TACTICAL FIREARMS – REFRESHER COURSE

The course is an annual course with 2 weeks' duration.

Aims

This consolidates what was first learned on the initial fire-arms course, including basic search and hostage situations. The handler and dog are also assessed on their abilities to work together on tactical firearms incidents. There will be role play incidents of hostage situations and practical exercise with regard to firearms and their use by the police.

Objectives

This course should ensure that the handler remains calm under stress and is consistent with this work with firearms. It also assesses the dog's understanding and capability for the tasks required through training exercises in buildings, open areas, vehicles and with armed police officers.

The handler has the opportunity to be made aware of any changes in the search techniques or the equipment used. He can also review incidents and discuss ideas with other officers, handlers and instructors.

HUMAN REMAINS DETECTION – INITIAL COURSE

This is a growing field of operation for which dogs are partic-ularly useful. The course lasts for up to 4 weeks, in addition to the general purpose course and the course on operational skills. The dog is trained to detect and indicate buried or concealed meat or bone in either a fresh or decomposed condition, and even when mummified.

Objectives

Through the completion of this course the handler is trained to handle a human remains detection dog. He personally must be self-motivated and conscientious with the ability to work without supervision. He should also be confident, patient and determined, with a good measure of common sense.

In order for the dog to be fit for this role, it must have an above average skill of searching and be capable of working in all conditions and areas. It also needs to have a good temperament, not nervous or aggressive. This type of dog needs to have stamina and be willing to work hard for long periods of time.

The handler must learn the correct way to work with a human remains detection dog as well as the correct method of searching. He must also be trained in field craft and the basics of decomposition of human remains and the environmental effect on these.

Dogs skilled in this work must be trained to obey its handler's commands correctly in order to detect and indicate human remains. They must be able to search in variety of places, indoors and out, and to ignore all distractions, including noise, movement and smells. They should also be willing to travel in various forms of transport.

HUMAN REMAINS DETECTION – REFRESHER COURSE

Aims

This course provides consolidation for the handler and dog of the skills required for searching and detecting. It usually covers one week every year. Simulated exercises give practical experience and enable assessment of skills.

Objectives

The competence of the handler in searching both indoor and outdoor areas is assessed, and the dog's competence in detecting buried or concealed meat or bone in fresh, decomposed or mummified states is tested.

The initial training of the dog is reinforced when the handler can provide positive searches as exercises to give the dog incentive for carrying out the task.

Handlers can also discuss the searches they have carried out and any problems encountered, as well as learning from each other and new information provided.

CONCLUSION

The work of a police dog handler is built on the close bond they have with their dog. Some dogs are matched with their handlers as puppies of about 12 weeks in order to forge the bond as soon as possible.

When they go through the police dog training course, they are prepared for any and all situations they may come up against. The dogs are trained according to their own natural instincts and their willingness to learn and obey their handler's commands. Each dog will have a particular skill that is their own, although all dogs have a general purpose built in, it seems, in order to aid and assist the police.

The basic obedience training teaches a dog to please and obey its pack leader, which, of course is, its handler. Once this is established, the partnership and relationship become very close.

The police dog is taught to bark continuously when he has found the object of a search, whether human or material.

He also learns to chase and detain or attack, even if he is threatened by a weapon.

There is a need for a police dog to be aggressive, but not vicious. It is of utmost importance that the dog obeys its handler always. Complete obedience is a necessity for a police dog. In whatever situation, the handler is always aware that he is to use only the necessary legal use of force in order to exert control. Therefore he must also control the limit of the use of his dog in certain situations and the commands that he gives it.

Once the weeks of basic training and operational skills are completed, refresher courses and training updates are required at intervals. A police dog will continue working with the same handler for 7 or 8 years and is then retired, usually continuing to live with its handler in his or her home. The handler will then begin the entire training process again with a new dog, which also will live with the handler and his retired dog.

If someone wants to train to become a police dog handler, he or she must first join the police force as a recruit. They are then required to at least complete their 2-year probationary training before applying to become a handler. However, many forces will only consider officers who have a few more years of experience on the job.

Once a candidate has been chosen to apply for training as a police dog handler, he has to complete a familiarisation course with his matched dog. The dog training staff then have to decide whether they are matched as a team and whether the candidate has what it takes to train as a handler. If he passes this first test, and if the dog is also considered suitable to become a police dog, the training begins.

The course is mentally and physically challenging. There is so much to learn and the subjects to be studied and practised are so varied, that there needs to be a great capacity for learning, both for the handler and for the dog. This is when the bond between the dog and the handler is really established, as they work together in learning and training.

Each dog has natural abilities and skills, according to their breed and characteristics. These are identified and built on. It can also be decided which particular job a dog may be more suited to, such as drugs or explosive detection, as well as general purpose duties. Instinct must be controlled and subject to command, so training is vital to the use of these natural abilities. Many of the exercise in police dog training are based on a dog's instincts and abilities, such as searching, retrieving, sniffing, detecting, guarding and controlling. Dogs assist in missing person searches, searching for criminals or property, locating drugs or explosives, hostage situations and crowd control.

Training is carried out with constant reward and praise for the dog. It is given complete care, exercise, feeding and protection by its handler, and its desire is to please its handler in everything he asks of it.

If both the dog and the handler achieve the required standards on their assessment at the end of the course, they are licensed to become operational together. It's then that the bond that was woven during training becomes deeper and more long lasting. Dogs and their handlers seem to know what each other is thinking and to be able to communicate without words. They have each been known to risk their life for the other, and in some instances one has sacrificed himself for the other, either man or dog.

Training is ongoing and is vital for the team of dog and

handler to remain at the cutting edge of law enforcement. They will be re-licensed every year after refresher courses. It's reassuring to know that these very committed teams patrol our streets and are there for the difficult and important times of life when only this close combination of man and dog can achieve such a result.

CHAPTER 9
THE LAWS FOR A POLICE DOG HANDLER

HUMAN RIGHTS ACT 1998

The first legal responsibility for a Police Dog Handler is to have due regard at all times to the Human Rights Act 1998, which includes:

- the right to life

- freedom from torture and degrading treatment

- freedom from slavery and forced labour

- the right to liberty

- the right to a fair trial

- the right not to be punished for something that wasn't a crime when you did it

- the right to respect for private and family life

 how2become

- freedom of thought, conscience and religion, and freedom to express your beliefs

- freedom of expression

- freedom of assembly and association

- the right to marry and to start a family

- the right not to be discriminated against in respect of these rights and freedoms

- the right to peaceful enjoyment of your property

- the right to an education

- the right to participate in free elections

- the right not to be subjected to the death penalty.

Each Police Force also has their own Human Rights Policy Statement to enforce these rights.

USE OF FORCE

When using Police Dogs, the Police Dog Handler must always be aware of the law on police use of force, which is set out in the Police and Criminal Evidence Act 1984.

The circumstances in which a Police Officer may use force are in:

"Self-defence, defence of another person or a property, prevention of a crime, or lawful arrest."

Only such force as is reasonable in the circumstances should be used, and it should be able to be justified that it was necessary. This is true both of the Police Officer himself and also his dog. The training that both officer and dog go through ensures that any use of force is considered reasonable. They

have a duty not to use force that might be considered inhuman and / or degrading treatment, as is stated in the Human Rights Act. Due to the Police and Criminal Evidence Act 1984 a Police Officer can use reasonable force if deemed necessary.

SIA LICENCE

Anyone who is a dog handler is legally required to have a Security Industry Authority (SIA) licence. The Police Dog Handler therefore must attend an approved training course, gain a nationally recognised qualification and undergo identity and CRB checks. They must also successfully complete a mandatory dog legislation course every year, which covers such subjects as the Human Rights Policy and the Dangerous Dogs Act 1991.

DEFRA

The Department of Environment, Food and Rural Affairs (Defra) publish leaflets regarding animals and their welfare, and anyone wanting to view the various Acts with regard to this can contact Defra as follows:

Defra Helpline: Telephone 08459 33 55 77
Email: helpline@defra.gsi.gov.uk

Please send general postal enquiries to:

DEFRA
Customer Contact Unit
Eastbury House
30 - 34 Albert Embankment
London
SE1 7TL

Or view the website: http://www.defra.gov.uk, where leaflets can be ordered or downloaded that give further information.

ACTS

Other legislation that the Police Dog Handler will need to know and abide by are included in the following Acts:

- Guard Dog Act 1975

- Dogs Act 1871

- Animals Act 1971

- Clean Neighbourhoods and Environments Act 2005

- Criminal Law Act 1967

- Police and Criminal Evidence Act 1984 (PACE)

- Firearms Act 1968

- Animal Welfare Act 2006

This act ensures owners and keepers are responsible for the welfare and needs of their animals: a suitable environment, diet, normal behaviour patterns, to be housed with, or apart from, other animals and to be protected from pain, injury, suffering and disease.

Police Dog Handlers are also subject to the Breeding of Dogs Act 1973, the Breeding of Dogs Act 1991 and the Breeding and Sale of Dogs (Welfare) Act 1999.

Dog Control Orders replaced Dog Byelaws in April 2006

Police Dog Handlers must also be aware of the Common Law, which has been established by the Courts. There is a responsibility to know that what they do in the carrying out of their duties is legal and cannot be called into question by anyone with whom they have to deal.

CHAPTER 10
POLICE DOG HANDLER FIT

HOW TO PLAN YOUR WORKOUT

Most people who embark on a fitness regime in January have given it up by February. The reason why most people give up their fitness regime so soon is mainly due to a lack of proper preparation. Preparation is key to your success and it is essential that you plan your workouts effectively.

Read on for some great ways to stay Police Dog Handler fit all year round!

What do you Want to Achieve?
The first step is to decide exactly what it is you want to achieve. Maybe you are attending the Police Officer Fitness test or you simply want to get in shape to make yourself feel healthier and fitter.

Whatever the reason your first step is to get a fitness test at the gym, weigh yourself and run your fastest mile. Once you have done all 3 of these steps write down your results

and keep them hidden away somewhere safe for one month. After a month of following your new fitness regime do all 3 tests again and check your results against the previous months. This is a great way to monitor your performance and progress.

Keep a Check on What you Eat and Drink.

Make sure you write down everything you eat and drink for a whole week. You must include tea, water, milk, biscuits and anything and everything that you digest. You will soon begin to realise how much you are eating and you will notice areas in which you can make some changes. For example, if you are taking sugar with your tea then why not try reducing it or giving it up all together. If you do then you will soon notice the difference.

It is important that you start to look for opportunities to improve your fitness and well being right from the offset.

You don't need a gym to get fit!

Walking is one of the best exercises you can do. If you don't have time to attend a gym then why not get up 30 minutes earlier in the morning and go on a brisk walk. Try doing this everyday for a week and see how you feel at the end of it - we guarantee you'll begin to feel healthier and fitter.

Also, walking is a fantastic way to lose weight if you think you need to. When we say walking we actually mean 'brisk' walking at a pace fast enough that you are not breaking out into a run or slow jog.

There are some great exercises contained within this guide and most of them can be carried out without the need to attend a gym.

One step at a time...

Try to set yourself small goals. If you think you need to lose 2 stone in weight then focus on losing a few pounds at a time, for example during your first month aim to lose 6 pounds. Once you have achieved this then again aim to lose 6 pounds over the next month, and so on and so forth.

The more realistic your goal, the more likely you are to achieve it. One of the biggest problems that people encounter when starting a fitness regime is that they become bored. This then leads to a lack of motivation and desire, and soon the fitness programme stops.

Change your exercise routine often. Instead of walking try jogging. Instead of jogging try cycling with the odd day of swimming. Keep your work outs varied and interesting to ensure that you stay focused and motivated.

STRETCHING EXERCISES

Why Stretch?
This area of fitness training and exercise is neglected by so many people. In fact if you fail to stretch properly before and after your exercise session you can increase your chances of injury dramatically. It is also very important to check with your GP that you are medically fit to carry out any form of physical exercise.

The Warm-Up Calf Stretch
Stand facing a wall with your right foot close to the wall and your right knee bent. Place your hands fl at against the wall at shoulder height. Now stretch your left leg out behind you as far as it will go, without lifting your toes and heel off the floor, and lean towards the wall. Hold for 10 to 30 seconds and relax.

Switch legs.

Shoulder Stretch
Stand with your feet slightly apart, your knees soft. Hold your arms out in front of you so that your palms are facing away from you. Now place your right palm on the back of your left hand and use it to push the left hand further away from you.

Switch sides.

Quad Stretch (Front of Thigh)
Stand with your right hand pressed against the back of a chair or a wall. Bend your left knee and bring your left heel up to your bottom, grasping your foot with your left hand. Your back should be straight and your shoulders, hips and knees should all be in line. Hold for 10 to 30 seconds.

Switch legs.

Hamstring Stretch (Back of Thigh)
Stand up straight and place your right foot onto a table, bench or chair so that your leg is almost parallel to the floor. Move your hands slowly down your right leg towards your ankle until you feel tension on the underside of your thigh. Try to lean forwards from the hips, keeping your back straight from the tailbone to the top of your head. Hold for 10 to 30 seconds.

Switch legs.

RUNNING PROGRAMME

WEEK 1
DAY 1

- Run a total of 3 miles only

If you cannot manage 3 miles then try the following:

- Walk at a brisk pace for half a mile or approximately 10 minutes;

Then

- Run for 1 mile or 8 minutes;

Then

- Walk for another half a mile or approximately 10 minutes;

Then

- Run for 1.5 miles or 12 minutes.

If you need to lose weight than walking at a brisk pace is possibly the most effective way to do so. It is possible to burn the same amount of calories if you walk the same distance as if you were running. When walking at a 'brisk' pace it is recommended that you walk as fast as is comfortably possible without breaking into a run or slow jog.

RUNNING PROGRAMME

WEEK 1
DAY 2

- Walk for 2 miles or approximately 20 minutes at a brisk pace; then

- Run for 2 miles or 14 minutes.

DAY 3

- Repeat DAY ONE.

DAY 4

- Walk at a brisk pace for 0.5 miles or approximately 7 minutes;

Then

- Run for 3 miles or 20 minutes.

DAY 5

- Repeat DAY ONE.

DAY 6 AND DAY 7

- REST DAYS – NO EXERCISE.

WEEK 2
DAY 1

- Run for 4 miles or 25 minutes.

DAY 2

- Run a total of 3 miles only. If you cannot manage 3 miles then try the following:

- Walk at a brisk pace for half a mile or approximately 10 minutes.

Then

- Run for 1 mile or 8 minutes.

Then

- Walk for another half a mile or approximately 10 minutes.

Then

- Run for 1.5 miles or 12 minutes.

DAY 3

- REST DAY – NO EXERCISE

DAY 4

- Run for 5 miles or 35 minutes.

DAY 5

- Run 3 miles or 20 minutes;

Then

- Walk at a brisk pace for 2 miles or approximately 20 minutes.

DAY 6

- Run for 5 miles or 35 minutes.

DAY 7

- REST DAY – NO EXERCISE.

RUNNING TIPS

- As with any exercise you should consult a doctor before taking part to make sure that you are medically fit.

- It is certainly worth investing in a pair of comfortable running shoes that serve the purpose for your intended training programme. Your local sports shop will be able to advise you on the type that is best for you. You don't have to spend a fortune to buy a good pair of running shoes.

- It is a good idea to invest in a 'high visibility' jacket or coat so that you can be seen by fast moving traffic if you intend to run on or near the road.

- Make sure you carry out at least 5 whole minutes of stretching exercise not only before but after your running programme. This can help to prevent injury.

- Whilst you shouldn't run on a full stomach it is also not good to run on an empty one either. A great food to eat approximately 30 minutes before a run is a banana. This is great for giving you energy.

- Drink plenty of water throughout the day. Try to drink at least 1.5 litres each day in total. This will keep you hydrated and help to prevent muscle cramp.

- Don't overdo it. If you feel any pain or discomfort then stop and seek medical advice.

PRESS UPS

Whilst running is a great way to improve your overall fitness you will also need to carry out exercises that improve your upper body strength. These exercises will help you to pass the dynamic strength tests that form part of the Police Selection process.

The great thing about press ups is that you don't have to attend a gym to perform them. However, you must ensure that you can do them correctly as injury can occur.

You may wish to spend just 5 minutes every day on press ups, possibly after you go running or even before if you prefer. If you are not used to doing press ups then begin slowly and aim to carry out at least 10.

Even if you struggle to do just 10 you will soon find that after a few days practice at these you will be up to 20+. Did you know that the world record for non stop press ups is currently 10,507 set in 1980!!!

WARNING – Ensure you take advice from a competent fitness trainer in relation to the correct execution of press up exercises.

SIT UPS

Lie flat on your back with your knees bent and your feet together fl at on the floor and about 10-15 inches from your buttocks. Your hands should either be crossed on your chest, by your side, or cupped behind your ears.

Without moving your lower body, curl your upper torso up and in toward your knees, until your shoulder blades are as high off the ground as you can get them.

Only your shoulder blades should lift and not your back.

As you come to the highest point tighten and flex your abdominals for a brief second.

Slowly lower yourself back to the starting position.

You should be aiming to work up to at least 50 effective sit ups every day. You will be amazed at how quickly this can be achieved and you will begin to notice your stomach muscles developing.

Whilst sit ups do not form part of the Police Fitness test they are still a great way of improving your all round fitness and therefore should not be neglected.

PULL UPS

As part of the selection process for joining the Police Force you will be required to take the bleep test or shuttle run test as it is otherwise called. Although running is the most effective way to prepare for the test you should not neglect your upper body fitness and strength as you will still need to successfully pass the Dynamic strength test.

Lateral pull downs or pull ups are very effective at increasing upper body strength. If you have access to a gymnasium

then these can be practised on a 'lateral pull down' machine. It is advised that you consult your gym member of staff to ask about these exercises.

If you do not have access to a gymnasium then you should make best use of the exercises contained within this guide to give yourself the best chance of passing the Police Fitness test. As previously mentioned press ups are a fantastic way of building up your upper body strength.

ALTERNATIVES TO THE GYM FOR BUILDING UPPER BODY STRENGTH

Apart from press ups, another fantastic way to improve your upper body and overall fitness is go swimming. If you have access to a swimming pool and you can swim then this is a brilliant way to improve your fitness.

If you are not a great swimmer you can start off with short distances and gradually build up your swimming strength and stamina.

Breast stroke is sufficient for building good upper body strength providing you put the effort into swimming an effective number of lengths. You may wish to alternate your running programme with the odd day of swimming.

If you can swim 10 lengths of a 25 metre pool initially then this is a good base to start from. You will soon find that you can increase this number easily providing that you carry on swimming every week.

Try running to your local swimming pool if it is not too far, swimming 20 lengths breast stroke, and then running home. This is a great way to combine your fitness activity and prevent yourself from getting bored of your programme.

THE POLICE OFFICER ENDURANCE TEST

You will find that during the Police fitness test you are required to pass the

Endurance Test or Bleep Test as it is otherwise known. The bleep test, which is also known as the multi-stage fitness test, is used by sports coaches and trainers to estimate an athlete's VO2 Max (maximum oxygen uptake). The test is especially useful for players of sports like football, hockey or rugby. The Police Force use this method of testing for their potential recruits and therefore you may find you will have to take this test during the selection process.

HOW TO PASS THE POLICE OFFICER ENDURANCE TEST

This part of the Police Officer selection process requires you to demonstrate a specific level of fitness. In simple terms the bleep test requires you to run backwards and forwards (shuttles) between 2 fixed points a set distance apart. The test is progressive in that as the levels increase so does the difficulty.

A tape will be played that contains a series of 'bleeps' set out at different intervals. The distance between the 'bleeps' at level 1 will be far greater than the 'bleeps' at level 10. Each time the 'bleeps' increase the tape will let you know that you are progressing to the next level. During the test you will be required to keep up with 'bleeps' and not fall behind them or run ahead of them. Level 1 starts off at around walking pace and gradually increases as each stage progresses.

The best way to practice for this stage of the test is to prac-tice the actual test itself. However, the next best alternative is to go running at least 3 miles, at least 3 times a week. Each time you go out running you should try to push yourself

a little bit harder and further.

By running 3 times a week you will give your body the rest it needs in between each run so it is probably best to run on alternate days. Please see our 'Running Programme' for tips and ideas.

EXERCISES

• Squats (work the legs and bottom).

Stand up straight with your arms at your sides or folded as indicated in the diagram below. Keep your feet shoulder-width apart and your head up. There can be a slight arch in your lower back. Slowly bend your knees while pushing your rear out as though you are about to sit down. Keep lowering yourself down until your thighs are almost parallel to the floor. Make sure your weight is on your heels so your knees don't extend over your toes. Tighten your thighs and buttocks for more of a challenge.

As you come back up to a standing position push down through your heels.

Repeat 10 to 15 times.

• Lunges (work the thighs and bottom).

Stand with your back straight and feet together (you may hold light hand weights if you're advanced). Inhale as you take a big step forward, landing with the heel first. Bend the front knee no more than 90 degrees.

Keep your back straight and lower the back knee as close to the floor as possible. Your front knee should be lined up over your ankle and your back thigh should be in line with your back. Exhale and push down against your front heel,

squeezing your buttocks tight as you rise back to a standing position.

Repeat 10 to 15 times. Switch sides.

• Chest press (works the chest).

Lie down on a bench with your feet resting comfortably on the floor. If you don't have a bench you can use a step or just lie down on the floor with your knees bent, feet flat on the floor. Extend your arms overhead, shoulder-width apart, palms facing your feet, so that the dumbbells (or tins of beans or small bottles of water) are positioned directly above your face and over your shoulders.

Gradually lower the weights out to the side until they're slightly above your shoulders. Your elbows should be bent at about 90 degrees so they almost touch the floor. Push the dumbbells up with an arcing motion until they're back in starting position.

Repeat 10 to 15 times.

• Press-ups (works the chest).

Kneel on the floor on all fours. Bend your arms and drop your chest forward and down towards the floor and inhale. Keeping your legs in the kneeling position, exhale as you push yourself up using your arms. Control the move by counting to three on the way up. As you push up, tighten your stomach muscles to take pressure off your back.

Hold for a second. Repeat 20 times.

• Lateral raise (works the shoulders)

Take a dumbbell in each hand and hold them by the sides of your body, palms facing inward. Stand or sit with your feet shoulder-width apart, knees slightly bent. Don't lean

backwards. Raise your arms up and out to the sides until they are parallel to the ground and then lower them back down.

Repeat 10 to 15 times.

STAYING WITH YOUR WORKOUT

In order to stay with your workout for longer try following these simple golden rules:

GOLDEN RULE ONE - work out often
Aim to train three to five times each week. Each training session should last between 20 minutes to an hour max. The quality of training is important so don't go for heavy weights but instead go for a lighter weight with a better technique. On days when you are feeling energetic take advantage of this opportunity to do more!

GOLDEN RULE TWO - Mix up your exercises
Your exercise programme should include some elements of cardiovascular (aerobics, running, brisk walking, skipping rope, rowing), resistance training(weights or own body exercises such as press ups) and, finally, flexibility (stretching).

Make sure that you always warm up and warm down. Try taking a class and if you are a member of a gym then why not take up a new class? For example a Pilate's class will teach you how to build core training into your exercise principles, and show you how to hit your abdominals in ways that are not possible with conventional sit-ups. You could even try kick-boxing...

GOLDEN RULE THREE - Eat a healthy and balanced diet
It is vitally important that you eat the right fuel to give you the energy to train to your full potential. Don't fill your body with rubbish and then expect to train well. Think about what you

are eating and drinking, including the quantities, and keep a record of what you are digesting. You will become stronger and fitter more quickly if you eat little amounts of nutritious foods at short intervals.

GOLDEN RULE FOUR - Get help

Try working with a personal trainer. They will ensure that you work hard and will help you to achieve your goals. If you cannot afford a personal trainer then try training with someone else. The mere fact that they are there at your side will add an element of competition to your training sessions! A consultation with a professional nutritionist will also help you improve your eating habits and establish your individual food needs.

GOLDEN RULE FIVE - Fitness is for life

Working out and eating correctly are not short-term projects. They are things that should be as natural to us as brushing our teeth. Make fitness a permanent part of your life by following these tips, and you'll lead a better and more fulfilling life.

BONUS I

POLICE DOG CONTACT DETAILS

If you would like to consider contacting your local Police Department about becoming a Police Officer and perhaps eventually a Police Dog Handler, or if you would like further information on Police Dogs and their work, you can either telephone or write to your local Police Department or look at their website. You may also wish to attend a Police Dog trial or show, or book a Police Dog Handler and his or her dog to attend a school or community function in order to learn more about their work. Below are just some of the contact details for a few of Police Departments and Dog Units around England, Scotland and Wales.

Devon & Cornwall Police / Dog Training School
Police Headquarters
Middlemoor
Exeter
Devon
EX2 7HQ
Tel: 08452 777 444

 how2become

Dumfries and Galloway Constabulary
Police Headquarters
Cornwall Mount
Dumfries
DG1 1PZ
Tel: 0845 600 5701
Email: fcc@dg.pnn.police.uk

Dyfed-Powys Police
Dog Section
Police Headquarters

PO Box 99
Carmarthen
SA31 2 PF
Tel: 0845 330 2000

Email: hqdogsectoin@dyfed-powys.police.uk

(They also run a lay visitors scheme which was started in 2001. It is a co-operation between the Dyfed Powys Police Authority, Dyfed Powys Police dog unit, the RSPCA, the Canine Defence League and representatives from the four County Councils. They also use volunteer puppy-walkers, ask for dog donations or re-homing for retiring police dogs.)

Lincolnshire Police
Police Headquarters
PO Box 999
Lincoln
NN5 7PH
Tel: 01522 532222

City of London Police
PO Box 36451
London
EC2M 4WN
Tel: 020 7601 2222

Norfolk Constabulary
Operations and Communications Centre
Jubilee House
Falconers Chase
Wymondham
Norfolk
NR18 0WW
Tel: 0141 531 5800

Northamptonshire Police
Tel: 08453 700700

Northern Constabulary
Police Dog Section
Inverness Area Command
Burnett Road
Inverness
IV1 1RL
Tel: 08456 033388

Web: www.northernconstabularycareers.co.uk

Strathclyde Police
Strathclyde Police Headquarters
173 Pitt Street
Glasgow
G2 4JS
Tel: 0141 532 2000

Strathclyde Dog Training Centre
Pollock County Park
Pollock
Glasgow
Tel: 0141 531 5800

Surrey Police Dog Training School
Surrey Police Headquarters
Mount Browne
Sandy Lane
Guildford
GU3 1HG
Tel: 0845 125 2222

Sussex Police
Malling House
Church Lane
Lewes
East Sussex
BN7 2DZ
Tel: 0845 6070999
Email: contact.centre@sussex.pnn.police.uk

Tayside Police
Force Headquaters
PO Box 59
West Bell Street
Dundee
DD1 9JU
Tel: 0300 111 2222
Email: mail@tayside.pnn.police.uk

The Wandsworth Parks Police

The Chief Officer
Parks Police
Battersea Park
London
SW11 4NJ
Tel: 020 8871 7532

Email: parkspolice@wandsworth.gov.uk

Police Dog Section:
Inspector Stephen Biggs, Head of Dog Section

Address and telephone as above
Email: sbiggs@wandsworth.gov.uk

John Bannerman, Chief Officer Parks Police
Address as above
Tel: 020 8871 7131

Email: jbannerman@wandsworth.gov.uk

West Midlands Police
Belgrave Road Police Station
Belgrave Middleway
Edgbaston
Birmingham
B5 7BP
Tel: 0845 113 5000

West Yorkshire Police
West Yorkshire Police Headquarters
PO Box 9
Wakefield
WF1 3QP
Tel: 0845 6060606

West Yorkshire Police Dog Training School
Tel: 01924 293135

You can sign up on some Police websites in order to receive updates on recruitment openings. Some Constabularies even have their own pages on Twitter or Facebook, where staff vacancies may be listed, as well as videos on YouTube of Police Dogs in training.

Other contact details that may be of interest, although not working with the Police, are as follows:

BGSD Dog Training School
Ebbw Vale
Gwent
South Wales

Security Industry Authority (SIA
PO Box 1293
Liverpool
L69 1AX
Tel: 0844 892 1025

Web: www.the-sia.org.uk

National Association of Security Dog Users (NASDU)
Web: www.nasdu.co.uk

National Search and Rescue Dog Association (NSARDA)
Web: www.nsarda.org.uk

Police Service Recruitment
Web: www.policecouldyou.co.uk
Web: www.policeservice.co.uk

HM Revenue and Customs (HMRC)
Web: www.hmrc.gov.uk

RAF Careers
Tel: 0845 605 5555

Web: www.rafcareers.com

British Army
Tel: 08457 300111

Web: www.army.mod.uk

Elite Canine Detection Solutions
The Fro
Glan Usk Estate
Crickhowell
Powys
NP8 1LP
Tel: 0873 812277

BONUS 2

USEFUL POLICE FORCE UK CONTACT DETAILS

Within this section we have provided you with Police Contact information including telephone numbers and website addresses (Internet connection required).

Contact the particular Police Force that you are interested in applying to join and see when they are recruiting.

A simple way to see whether the force of your choice is recruiting or not is to visit the Police Could You website which can be found at www.policecouldyou.co.uk.

If your particular force is not recruiting at the present time then it is worthwhile calling them to find out when they anticipate recruiting next. You can use this time wisely to help you to prepare for the pending recruitment drive. This will also give you some indication as to whether you wish to apply for a Police Force out of your home County area and then apply to transfer to your home one at a later date.

NORTH EAST REGION

CLEVELAND POLICE
Telephone: 01642 301 479
www.cleveland.police.uk

DURHAM POLICE
Telephone: 0191 3752125
www.durham.police.uk

HUMBERSIDE POLICE
Telephone: 01482 220 096
www.humberside.police.uk

NORTHUMBRIA POLICE
Telephone: 01661 868 816
www.northumbria.police.uk

NORTH YORKSHIRE POLICE
Telephone: 01609 789 079
www.northyorkshire.police.uk

WEST YORKSHIRE POLICE
Telephone: 01924 292 069
www.westyorkshire.police.uk

SOUTH YORKSHIRE POLICE
Telephone: 0114 282 1234
www.southyorkshire.police.uk

NORTH WEST REGION

CHESHIRE POLICE
Telephone: 01244 614 021
www.cheshire.police.uk

CUMBRIA POLICE
Telephone: 01768 217 092
www.cumbria.police.uk

GREATER MANCHESTER POLICE
Telephone: 0161 856 2333
www.gmp.police.uk

LANCASHIRE POLICE
PO Box 77Hutton
Nr. Preston
Lancashire
PR4 5SB
www.lancashire.police.uk

MERSEYSIDE POLICE
Telephone: 0151 777 8238
www.merseyside.police.uk

WALES POLICE
DYFED POWYS POLICE
Telephone: 01267 222020
www.dyfed-powys.police.uk

GWENT POLICE
Telephone: (01495) 745407/745409
www.gwent.police.uk

NORTH WALES POLICE
Telephone: 01492 510019
www.north-wales.police.uk

SOUTH WALES POLICE
Telephone: 01656 869225
www.south-wales.police.uk

MIDLANDS POLICE

WARWICKSHIRE POLICE
Telephone: 01926 415052
www.warwickshire.police.uk

WEST MERCIA POLICE
Telephone: 01905 723 000
www.westmercia.police.uk

WEST MIDLANDS POLICE
Telephone: 0121 626 5824
www.west-midlands.police.uk

LEICESTERSHIRE POLICE
Telephone: 0116 222 2222 ext. 2657
www.leics.police.uk

NORTHANTS POLICE
Telephone: 01604 703 091
www.northants.police.uk

STAFFORDSHIRE POLICE
Telephone: 01785 235353
www.staffordshire.police.uk

SOUTH WEST POLICE

AVON AND SOMERSET POLICE
Telephone: 01275 816142
www.avonandsomerset.police.uk

DEVON AND CORNWALL POLICE
Telephone: 01392 452500
www.devon-cornwall.police.uk

DORSET POLICE
Telephone: 01305 223 794
www.dorset.police.uk

GLOUCESTERSHIRE POLICE
Telephone: 0845 090 1234
www.gloucestershire.police.uk

WILTSHIRE POLICE
Telephone: 01380 722 341
www.wiltshire.police.uk

SOUTH EAST POLICE

METROPOLITAN POLICE
Telephone: 0845 727 2212 (8am-6pm)
www.metpolicecareers.co.uk

SURREY POLICE
Telephone: 01483 482266
www.surrey.police.uk

SUSSEX POLICE
Telephone: 01273 404 151
www.sussex.police.uk

THAMES VALLEY POLICE
Telephone: 01865 846 816
www.thamesvalley.police.uk

BRITISH TRANSPORT POLICE
Telephone: 020 7388 9121
www.btp.police.uk

EASTERN POLICE

CAMBRIDGESHIRE POLICE
Telephone:0845 456 456 4
www.cambridgeshire.police.uk

DERBYSHIRE POLICE
Telephone: 01773 572104
www.derbyshire.police.uk

LINCOLNSHIRE POLICE
Telephone: 01522 558235
www.lincolnshire.police.uk

NORFOLK POLICE
Telephone: 01953 423823
www.norfolk.police.uk

NOTTINGHAMSHIRE POLICE
Telephone: 0115 967 2424
www.nottinghamshire.police.uk

SUFFOLK POLICE
Telephone: 01473 613 640
www.suffolk.police.uk

SCOTTISH POLICE

CENTRAL SCOTLAND POLICE
Tel: +44 (0)1786 456000
Fax: +44 (0)1786 451177
Text-telephone: +44 (0)1786 445533
www.centralscotland.police.uk

DUMFRIES AND GALLOWAY POLICE
Telephone: 01387 252112
Fax: 01387 260501
www.dumfriesandgalloway.police.uk

FIFE CONSTABULARY
Telephone: 01592 418888
www.fife.police.uk

GRAMPIAN POLICE
Telephone: 0845 6005700
www.grampian.police.uk

LOTHIAN AND BORDERS POLICE
Telephone: 0131 311 3131
www.lbp.police.uk

Attend a 1-Day intensive Police Officer training course run by former serving Police Officers.

Visit the following website for more details:

www.PoliceCourse.co.uk

how2become

Visit www.how2become.co.uk to find more titles and courses that will help you to pass the police officer selection process:

- Online police officer testing

- 1 Day police officer training course

- Police officer books and DVD's

- Psychometric testing books and CDs.

www.how2become.co.uk